"…will help you walk the path of conscious living towards a life of greater vitality."

—**GAY HENDRICKS**
author of *Conscious Living*

"Irresistible…A must-do workbook for anyone looking to realize his/her full potential."

—**MICHELLE TURCHIN**
Director of Human Resources, Wildlife Conservation Society

"This is a very fun, very useful guide to taking your personal impact and contributions to a higher level. I love the tools and practical advice."

—**KEVIN D. WILDE**
Chief Learning Officer, General Mills

Stop the busywork, and start the work that matters.

P9-CRF-372

Michael Bungay Stanier, named Canadian Coach of the Year in 2006, is the founder and senior partner of Box of Crayons, a company that helps organizations make the leap from good work to Great Work. He lives in Toronto, and his website is *www.BoxOfCrayons.biz.*

Do More Great Work.

Stop the busywork, and start the work that matters.

MICHAEL BUNGAY STANIER

WORKMAN PUBLISHING, NEW YORK

To my outstanding nieces and nephews—Mathilde, Harper, George, Seamus, and Hendrix—and to my godson, Finlay, and goddaughter, Stella.

Library of Congress Cataloging-in-Publication Data is available

ISBN 978-0-7611-5644-4

Art direction by David Matt
Design by Sara Edward-Corbett

I♥
NY © 2010 NYSDED. All rights reserved. I LOVE NEW YORK is a registered trademark and service mark of NYSDED.

Workman books are available at special discount when purchased in bulk for premiums and sales promotions as well as for fund-raising or educational use. Special editions or book excerpts also can be created to specification. For details, contact the Special Sales Director at the address below.

Workman Publishing Company, Inc.
225 Varick Street
New York, NY 10014-4381
www.workman.com

Printed in the United States of America
First Printing January 2010
10 9 8 7 6 5 4 3 2

Acknowledgments

THANK *YOU*. For you to pick up this book, read it, use it—that's a commitment and a gift of time and energy, and I appreciate it.

Marcella, my wife and the VP of Everything Else, you are a constant source of inspiration, challenge, and love, and having you in my life is indeed Great Work. Thank you for all the research, proofreading, and feedback you provided for this particular project.

This book is enriched by the contributions of some smart, provocative, and wise people. Leo Babauta, Seth Godin, Chris Guillebeau, Tim Hurson, Michael Port, Penelope Trunk, and Dave and Wendy Ulrich all found time in their busy lives to write something original and unique for this book. Thank you all.

Thank you to the fantastic members of the Box of Crayons team: Ana Garza-Robillard, Robert Kabwe, Jill Morton, Ernest Oriente, Kathryn Presner, Charlotte Riley, Sue Seybert, and all the Coaching for Great Work program leaders.

Do More Great Work is a revised and expanded version of the self-published *Find Your Great Work*. My debt to the many people who made it happen—friends, newsletter readers, clients, and peers—is set out in full in that book.

Thank you, Nick and Wendy Boothman, who pushed open the door at Workman, and thank you Peter Workman, Suzie Bolotin, and the full team at Workman who welcomed me most graciously. In particular, thank you Margot Herrera, who as my editor did a fantastic job in ensuring there were absolutely no flabby bits, at the same time encouraging me to step around my bias toward brevity. Much gratitude also goes to Sara Edward-Corbett and David Matt for design, Beth Levy for her attention to detail, and Kristin Matthews, Oleg Lyuber, Melissa Possick, and Andrea Fleck-Nisbet for helping to bring attention to the book.

Thank you to the writers and thinkers who've provoked and inspired me over the years, not just for what they've said but also for how they've said it and made it known in the world. In what is certainly an incomplete list, I'd acknowledge: David Allen, Octavius Black, Peter Block, Bill Bryson, Martin Buber, Marcus Buckingham, Italo Calvino, Richard Carson, Jim Collins, David Cooperrider, Ben Dean, Deborah Ford, Tim Gallwey, Malcolm Gladwell, Milton Glaser, Seth Godin, Marshall Goldsmith, Michael Grinder, Bill Jensen, Robert Kegan, Peter Koestenbaum, Michael Leunig, Adam Morgan, Mary Beth O'Neill, Tom Peters, Dick Richards, David Rock, Marshall Rosenberg, Edgar Schein, Susan Scott, Jerry Sternin, Ben Zander, and Theodore Zeldin.

Thank you to a number of clients who've been loyal and encouraging beyond the call of duty. In particular, I'd like to acknowledge Anne Mueller of AstraZeneca; Bob Presner and Lola Rasminsky of Beyond the Box; Laura Walker of British Gas; Michael Leckie of Gartner Inc.; Mark Peters of Nestlé; and Kathy Conway, Carl Oxholm, and Chris Gillespie of PricewaterhouseCoopers.

And to end where I began, thank you again, Marcella.

Contents

Here's the Challenge

You spend more than half your life at work. And you want your work to make an impact and have a purpose, to be more than just a salary. You want to make it count.

But that keeps getting lost. You know you could be doing more work that's meaningful for you and useful for your organization—yet somehow all the other stuff keeps getting in the way.

So how do you do more of the work that engages and stretches you—so you continue to grow and don't get stuck in a rut? How do you increase your personal contribution—so your work actually has an impact? How do you play to your strengths—so you're doing what you're best at? In short, how do you do more of the work that makes a difference and makes you happy, and less of all that other stuff that somehow fills your working day?

Right now it's not that easy to do Great Work. We're stretched to capacity, and we spend our time rushing from meeting to meeting, just trying to process the tasks coming our way. Technology keeps

Do More Great Work.

us overconnected and ever busy, as if *busy* were somehow a measure of success. The ebb and flow of the economy makes us feel less certain about the future, so we cling to what we know, as if that were all it takes to be secure.

This book is the sum of my work with thousands of people around the world as a coach and a facilitator. It uses just fifteen key tools—conceptual maps to help you identify what really matters to you, what drives the choices and the actions you take, and how you can get onto a path to more creative, motivated, and inspired work that's good for you and good for those you work for. The exercises are simple, quick to do, and deeply practical, and they help you focus on a Great Work Project so you can do more Great Work. Throughout the book you'll also find Great Work thoughts from smart people. And not just any smart people. Leo Babauta writes the world's most popular productivity blog, Dave

Ulrich is a leading HR guru, Chris Guillebeau is a champion for the art of nonconformity, Tim Hurson is an innovation whiz, Michael Port's a business marketing guru, Penelope Trunk leads a tribe for Gen Y at work, and Seth Godin writes quite possibly the best business books in the world. These contributions are like Pop Rocks candy for your brain—each one fizzes and stimulates and delights.

You don't need a coach or a shrink or a consultant or a weekend retreat to figure out how to do more Great Work. You just need a pen, some paper, and a little bit of time to get clear on what matters and to build your own plan to do it. You also need to say, "It's time"—and get going.

Have more impact. Make more of a difference. Be happier. Do more Great Work.

Warm wishes,

Michael

Michael Bungay Stanier

PART I

Laying the Foundation

INTRODUCTION

Before You Get Going . . .

I f you don't know where you're starting from, it can be tough to get to where you want to go.

Most of this book is dedicated to getting you on a path to doing more Great Work. But before that happens, let's spend just a moment or two figuring out where you are now.

We're going to start by having a close look at exactly what Great Work is. I don't want you feeling that Great Work is beyond your reach, that it's only for people who already have a deep sense of mission, who have reached enlightenment, or who are somehow extraordinary. Everyone can do more Great Work.

In this section, I'm going to explain why I call the exercises "maps" and share four tips that will help you use them to their full effect. Then I'm going to suggest three things you can do before you embark on the process that will make it easier to succeed. And finally I'll share the first of the fifteen maps. This initial map sets the scene by helping you figure out how much Great Work you're doing now—something that's useful to know before you set out on a journey to do more of it.

JUST WHAT IS (AND ISN'T) GREAT WORK?

Graphic designer Milton Glaser started this ball rolling for me. Even if you've never heard of him, you probably know his most famous creation: I LOVE NEW YORK.

His book *Art is Work* is mainly a collection of his design work, but he opens it with a curious and powerful insight. He says everything we do falls into three basic categories:

Bad Work • Good Work • Great Work.

YOU ALREADY KNOW WHAT THESE CATEGORIES MEAN

Over the years, I've asked thousands of people at hundreds of different organizations what these categories mean to them. Intuitively, they know—and their answers can be summed up like this:

Bad Work

Bad Work is a waste of time, energy, and life. Doing it once is one time too many. This is not something to be polite about. It's not something to be resigned to. This is work that is pointless.

Sadly, organizations have a gift for generating Bad Work. It shows up as bureaucracy, interminable meetings, outdated processes that waste everyone's time, and other ways of doing things that squelch you rather than help you grow.

Good Work

Good Work is the familiar, useful, productive work you do—and you likely do it well. You probably spend most of your time on Good Work, and there's nothing wrong with that. Good Work blossoms from your training, your education, and the path you've traveled so far. All in all, it's a source of comfort, nourishment, and success.

There's a range of Good Work: At one end it's engaging and interesting work; at the other, it is more mundane but you recognize its necessity and are happy enough to spend some time doing it.

You always need Good Work in your life. At an organizational level, Good Work is vital. It is a company's bread and butter—the efficient, focused, profitable work that delivers next quarter's returns.

Great Work

Great Work is what we all want more of. This is the work that is meaningful to you, that has an impact and makes a difference. It inspires, stretches, and provokes. Great Work is the work that matters.

It is a source of both deep comfort and engagement—often you feel as if you're in the "flow zone," where time stands still and you're working at your best, effortlessly. The comfort comes from its connection, its "sight line," to what is most meaningful to you—not only your core values, and beliefs, but also your aspirations and hopes for the impact you want to have on the world.

But Great Work is also a place of uncertainty and discomfort. The discomfort arises because the work is often new and challenging, and so there's an element of risk and possible failure. Because this is work that matters, work that you care about, you don't want it to fail. But because it's new and challenging, there's a chance that it might.

For organizations, Great Work drives strategic difference, innovation, and longevity. Often it's the kind of inventive work that pushes business forward, that leads to new products, more efficient systems, and increased profits.

> All great deeds and all great thoughts have a ridiculous beginning. Great works are often born on a street corner or in a restaurant's revolving door.
>
> *ALBERT CAMUS*

SO FAR, SO GOOD

Those are three fairly straightforward definitions. You're probably nodding your head and thinking, "Yep, I get that." But how do you get the balance right? What's your perfect mix?

The truth is there is no perfect mix. Finding the right mix between your Good Work and Great Work (with no Bad Work) is the practice of a lifetime. And even if you do find a harmonious balance now, it will change. The best mix for this year won't be right twelve months later.

A number of factors account for this:

1. **Great Work decays.** Over time, Great Work decays into Good Work. As Great Work becomes comfortable and familiar as you master it, it no longer provides the challenge, stretch, or rewards it once did. Your Great Work of today won't be your Great Work five years from now.

   The iPod syndrome kicks in. Remember how special iPods were when they first arrived on the scene? Now everyone has one, and they're taken for granted.

2. **Good Work has its attractions.** Even as we hunger for more Great Work, we're always drawn back to the comfort of Good Work. It's a perpetual tension—the challenge, risk, and reward of the Great against the familiarity, efficiency, and safety of the Good.

3. **Different years demand different responses.** Some years are "stretch" years when you go for it; others are years to conserve your strength, gathering ideas and laying the groundwork for your next initiative. This ebb and flow reminds me of an anniversary card I once saw that read, "Thanks for 20 great years . . . 7 average years . . . and 2 absolute stinkers."

But here's one thing I bet you've never said: "I have too much Great Work." Because no one says, "My life's just too interesting, too stimulating, too engaging, too fulfilling, too provocative. . . ." No one says, "I don't want to do more Great Work."

In fact whatever your mix might currently be, almost inevitably you're hungry for more Great Work. And that's how these fifteen maps can help.

> I have an existential map. It has "You are here" written all over it.
>
> *STEVEN WRIGHT*

THE POWER OF MAPS

In this book, there are fifteen tools that will help you find and do more Great Work. They're designed to reveal how you're working now, help you decide what you'd like to do differently, and instill the energy, drive, and confidence you need to do something about it. I call them maps for two reasons:

Maps help you ask and answer questions. We live in a culture that makes us do, do, do, with an emphasis on moving forward without really considering our path. Maps encourage us to stop and ask deep, powerful questions, like:

▶ Where am I?
▶ How did I get here?
▶ Where am I going?
▶ Is there a better route?
▶ Could there be a different destination?

Maps don't just provide a new view of the landscape. They can also be a pause button in disguise. And sometimes taking some time to size things up is the most important thing you can do.

Do More Great Work.

Maps help you take action. They provoke you to make some fundamental choices that become the basis for action.

- ▶ Do I keep going?
- ▶ Do I stop?
- ▶ Do I take a new direction?

With the new perspective that a map brings, it's impossible not to make choices and do something—even if you choose to "keep on keepin' on" or even to do nothing for now.

FOUR TIPS TO HELP YOU MAKE THE MOST OF THE MAPS

1. **Make the maps yours.** Another reason maps are powerful is because they demand interaction from the person using them. The maps in this book are useless without your input. It is the information you bring to each that will make it relevant and timely for you.

   The maps aren't static. You can (and should) revisit each one. You'll likely discover that it will have changed. The map you create in August will be different from the one you do in January. In fact, revisiting the maps is in itself a useful exercise, as it can offer new perspectives as well as help you track your progress in doing Great Work.

2. **Find five minutes in your day.** The good news is that you don't need to go on a three-day retreat to find the time to do these exercises. While there's deep thinking and theory behind the maps, they're also designed so you can work with each of them in five minutes or less. After all, most maps are designed to impart practical information in a quick, accessible way.

   All you need is a pen, a sheet of paper, and the willingness to take a few minutes to think about what matters to you. If you do, then this book will give you structures and insights with which to do more Great Work. So while you're eating lunch, waiting for a teleconference to start, or riding the train back home, pick up the book and play with a map. (You can of course spend as long as you'd like working on the maps. There's certainly a benefit to giving yourself some real time to reflect on Great Work.)

3. **Use the maps in the order that makes sense to you.** There's a method to how the maps are arranged.

The first map helps establish where you are now and how much Great Work you're doing. Maps 2, 3, and 4 help you figure out what might be Great Work for you. Maps 5, 6, and 7 shift the focus from you to where the opportunities lie to do more Great Work. Map 8 guides you in choosing a Great Work project and 9, 10, and 11 help you expand the possibilities you have before you and then evaluate them in anticipation of taking action. Maps 12, 13, and 14 launch you into your Great Work and help you to determine the next steps necessary for moving forward. The very last map keeps you on track when the going gets rough.

The maps are designed to build on each other so you can work through them systematically and end up with a specific plan to do more Great Work. But really, how you use them is entirely up to you. Feel free to pick and choose. Find a map that seems to answer your immediate need, fill it out, and see where it leads you.

> Your work is going to fill a large part of your life, and the only way to be truly satisfied is to do what you believe is great work. And the only way to do great work is to love what you do. If you haven't found it yet, keep looking. Don't settle. As with all matters of the heart, you'll know when you find it.
>
> *STEVE JOBS*

No matter what order you do them in, I'd encourage you to work through them all at some point.

4. Don't worry about getting it perfect. You may have heard that when ancient mapmakers ran up to the very edge of the known world, they would write *Hic sunt dracones,* or "Here there be dragons." While that occurs far more in fantasy novels than it does in actual cartography, what is true is that in filling out the maps, you *will* run up against the edges of what you know and what you can anticipate. You won't always (or ever) have all the information and be able to map out everything fully.

Or you might find yourself thinking that your map is wrong. Of course it is. In fact, there's no such thing as a correct map. "The map," philosopher Alfred Korzybski once said, "is not the territory." Your map isn't reality; it's only your best guess at describing it.

That's OK. In fact, one of the reasons why you create a map in the first place is to discover what you don't know, as well as what you do. In short, an incomplete map is useful because often it is the gaps that spark questions and spur you to action.

> The thing that is really hard, and really amazing, is giving up on being perfect and beginning the work of becoming yourself.
>
> *ANNA QUINDLEN*

The real test? Ask yourself if this map is useful for you now. Does it give you a new insight on how to do more Great Work? Does it help you to do anything differently? If so, then it's serving its purpose. If not, then make a change—add some new data to the map, come back to it later, or even just move on to another map.

Six Great Work Paradoxes

Or you could call this section "Six reasons why you might already be giving up on the idea of Great Work—and why you shouldn't."

I. YOU DON'T NEED TO SAVE THE WORLD. YOU DO NEED TO MAKE A DIFFERENCE.

The desire to do more Great Work is not a call to abandon your everyday life and become a martyr to a cause. You don't need to quit your job, stop earning money, give up your friends, or cease wearing regular clothes. Nor do you need to start a global movement, overthrow governments, or spark a revolution.

But it *is* a call to do more meaningful work. What can you do more of that makes a difference, shifts the balance, has an impact, adds beauty, changes the status quo, creates something worth being created, improves life, moves things forward, reduces waste, engages people, or allows love? (You don't have to do all of those. Just one will be fine.) There are opportunities to do any of these things all around you right now. Maps 5 and 6 will help you find them.

2. GREAT WORK IS PRIVATE. GREAT WORK CAN BE PUBLIC.

It can be nice to get the applause, win the medal, or receive the pat on the back that says, *Well done!* And sometimes Great Work generates just that sort of recognition.

But not always. Because it is a subjective matter—Great Work is what is meaningful for *you*—often its reward is a moment of private triumph. Maps 2, 3, and 4 will help you define exactly what it is that matters to you. You know you've done something that matters, ▶

something that raised the bar a little, something that stretched you in certain ways—but not everyone else will know it. In fact, if you're just after public acclaim, then doing Great Work might not even be the best route.

3. GREAT WORK IS NEEDED. GREAT WORK ISN'T WANTED.

What calls you to do Great Work is often a feeling of *I can't take it anymore. I've got to do something different.* It's a personal sense that something needs to be done, that the status quo can't be tolerated any longer, and that you need to be the one to adjust it. Great Work shows up at the intersection where what needs to change in your world meets what's important to you.

But Great Work is often not wanted. Oh, sure, it might well be *talked about* as wanted. Corporate leaders, in particular, are experts at proclaiming some sort of Great Work as the next quest for their organizations. But most organizations are deeply rooted in delivering Good Work and sustaining the way things are, so that there's minimal interruption to that Good Work. Taking a stand for Great Work means in some small (or significant) way swimming against the tide. Maps 7 and 11 will help you step up to this challenge.

4. GREAT WORK IS EASY. GREAT WORK IS DIFFICULT.

Sometimes when you're doing Great Work, it's a glorious thing. You're in that flow zone where things come easily and time seems suspended.

Everything that is contradictory creates life.

SALVADOR DALÍ

But not always. In fact, not even necessarily most of the time.

Great Work can be a time of grinding through it, of showing up when your muse isn't whispering to you. It can be a time of uncertainty, groping forward when you're not sure of where you're heading. It can mean picking yourself up off the floor and carrying on after the unexpected has just slapped you around a bit.

There are times when doing Great Work will test you. It will call on not just your skills and talents, but your resilience and your ability to manage yourself through the dip. Maps 14 and 15 may be able to help you with that.

5. GREAT WORK IS ABOUT DOING WHAT'S MEANINGFUL. GREAT WORK ISN'T ABOUT DOING IT WELL.

Here's the irony: It's often easy to deliver Bad Work and Good Work at an excellent level. (Just how many times have you revised that worthless PowerPoint presentation?)

And Great Work? It's often new work at the edge of your competence, work that tangles you up because it's different and you haven't done it a thousand times before. You're unlikely to be able to do it perfectly. When I say "Great Work," I'm not talking about a standard of delivery. I'm talking about a standard of impact and meaning.

6. GREAT WORK CAN TAKE A MOMENT. GREAT WORK CAN TAKE A LIFETIME.

Great Work can happen in a single moment. It's a time when you feel at your best, achieving a personal triumph, the culmination of days or weeks or years of practice.

Great Work can also be a project that develops over time, something that you've started and seen through. Not every minute of the journey is Great Work, but what it adds up to is.

Great Work can also take a lifetime. It can be a commitment to making changes in yourself and your world by means of the work that you do, or it can be a connection to a cause that pulls you forward and helps you be who you want to be. Somehow, time can both shrink and stretch to accommodate a Great Work moment.

These definitions are all true. They're all equally important. ∎

ARE YOU UP FOR THE CHALLENGE?

You're getting ready to go on a journey of sorts, a journey to find and do more Great Work.

All books like this are an invitation to start something new, try a different approach, and step into a new way of working and living. I don't know about you, but here's how I typically respond to that call to action. I pick up the book in question, flip through it, think, *Ah, that's a cool insight,* or *Hmm . . . , interesting,* or maybe *I should try that sometime.*

Maybe I get to the end of the book, maybe I don't. But eventually I put the book back on the shelf—and very little has changed.

I'd love this book to be different, to actually help you make a change in what you're doing now so you can do more Great Work.

Here are three things you might like to consider so as to be best prepared for what's ahead.

1. **Get committed.** Answer this question right now: Just how committed are you to doing Great Work? What's your score on a scale of 1 to 10, with 10 being totally committed? Are you at 7? 4? 9? Something else?

   Think about that score. What's the implication for how you're about to read and use this book? Are you going to flip through the pages, and then put it aside? Do you think you might try out one or two of the exercises just to see what comes up? Will you try all the exercises and hope for positive change but not count on it?

   Where do you stand right now?

   And finally, if you were fully committed, scoring a big 10 out of 10 on the commitment meter, what would be different? How would you use this book and this opportunity if that were the case?

> The reinvention of daily life means marching off the edge of our maps.
>
> *BOB BLACK*

2. Get a notebook. You'll find this isn't a typical book in that I won't be going on and on for pages at a time, sharing my views of the world and telling you what to do. It's much more like a workbook. I provide you with some useful structures, frameworks, and questions, and you get to work with them to help make sense of your life and start to do more Great Work.

You can make notes directly in this book, if you like. But you might want to consider getting yourself a notebook devoted to jotting down insights, thoughts, and ideas, practicing the exercises, and planning how to do more Great Work.

> Though no one can go back and make a brand new start, anyone can start from now and make a brand-new ending.
>
> *CARL BARD*

A notebook will be useful because these exercises are perennial. You can come back to them time and time again, and they'll always offer something new, useful, and insightful. Being able to track how your thinking and doing has changed over time will be both interesting and valuable.

3. Get a buddy. Winnie the Pooh, that bear of great wisdom, once said, "It's so much more friendly with two." And so it is.

But it's not just more friendly. It's also more likely that you'll actually do something differently. (You know in your bones how difficult it is to implement the suggestions you read in a book.)

Consider finding a Great Work buddy and supporting each other in working through the exercises. Ask a friend, a work colleague, or someone you know online. It doesn't matter where—just find one.

Then check in with each other regularly. Be encouraging—but kick each other's butt when you don't do what you want to do.

MAP 1

Where Are You Now?

To get to a destination, you need to know
your starting point

ONE OF THE MIRACLES OF the Internet age is Google Maps. No longer
do you have to haul out a slightly out-of-date road atlas to plot your journey
from point A to point B. You just type in your destination, and your journey is
plotted for you, with helpful tips, if you want them, on where to stop for coffee.
But it works only if you know your starting point. Without that it's impossible
to create a plan to get to a destination.

YOUR STARTING POINT A

This first map will give you a snapshot of a moment in time—now—that
will help you see what your current work mix looks like. Once you're clear
on this, you can start to define just what your destination might be and how
you're going to get there.

MAP 1: WHERE ARE YOU NOW?

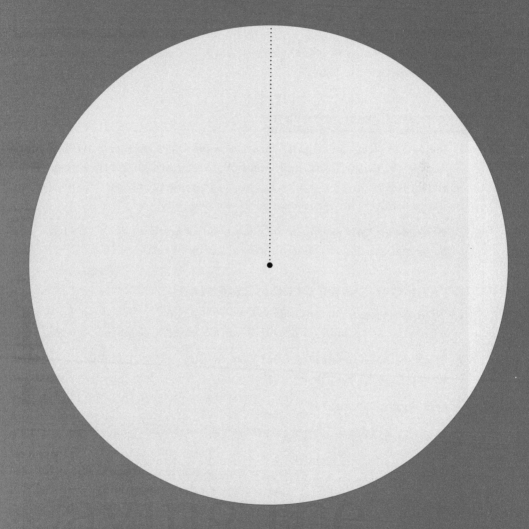

Do More Great Work.

So, knowing that there are only three types of work—Bad, Good, and Great—and knowing that you're doing a certain amount of each right now, how much of each are you doing?

COMPLETING THE MAP

1. **Divide the circle on page 17 into three pie slices representing how much Bad Work, Good Work, and Great Work you are currently doing.** Trust your intuition on this—you don't have to be overly precise. And by the way, the proportions are almost certainly *not* one third each.

2. **Write down two examples of each type of work in each segment.** This helps make it clear to yourself just what you're talking about.

GETTING INSIGHTS FROM THE MAP

1. **What does your current mix tell you?** How do you feel about how things are? What are you happy about? What are you disappointed about?

2. **What would your ideal mix be?** How would you like the map to look? Most people want no Bad Work and more Great Work, but the mix of Good and Great varies from person to person and from time to time. This "gap analysis"—where you are now as compared to where you want to be—will help provide some of the impetus to make changes, and also give you clues as to what work you might want to stop doing, continue doing, and start doing.

If you're interested in the bigger picture, I've asked people from around the world, and most say

> If you don't change your beliefs, your life will be like this forever. Is that good news?
>
> *DOUGLAS ADAMS*

their percentages in the three work categories currently fall somewhere within these ranges:

▶ 10–40 percent Bad Work
▶ 40–80 percent Good Work
▶ 0–25 percent Great Work

If your mix is different, don't worry. This is just a snapshot of what you see now. In six months, your mix will most likely be different—especially if you've been putting this book to good use!

FOR EXAMPLE . . .

Andy leads a marketing team in one of the global pharmaceutical companies. They're gearing up for a new product launch in the next six months, and it's a busy time for everyone.

Andy had led such teams before in his previous company—he's been at this company less than eighteen months—but never one quite this complex. Not only is the team of twelve larger than any he's ever worked with, but more than half of the group works at different sites in different countries, spanning multiple time zones.

Going into this exercise, Andy was pretty certain that his Great Work would be the launch of the product. It promised to help people live better lives, and he was excited to make the project extraordinary. He had envisioned a committed team building a creative, powerful marketing strategy that would not only excite the senior leaders of the company and the sales force but also capture the imaginations of their customers and trump the rival product.

However, the project wasn't going as well as it might. The members of his team were having trouble coming up with a viable strategy, and there were tensions among the team members. Andy was struggling to get them and the project back on track.

When Andy completed this map, he was a little disappointed at what he found. Only a sliver, about 10 percent, was Great Work—the actual marketing thinking he was doing about the project. About 60 percent of his time was devoted to Good Work, which included moving the project along, working with the other parts of the business involved in the launch, and most of his other day-to-day work responsibilities. The remaining 30 percent was Bad Work. Some of it was "administrivia," but a good part of it was managing what he called the "delicate egos" on his team.

Doing the exercise caused a number of insights to start to percolate for Andy:

▶ His Great Work—the innovative marketing thinking—was something that he loved, but his opportunity for doing it was much reduced now that he was leading the team. He had others on the team whose role it was to lead the crafting of the marketing strategy, and it would be difficult to do more of this without stepping on their toes.

▶ He'd never felt comfortable assuming a strong leadership role. He'd hoped the team would just sort of figure it out and do what needed to be done. Unfortunately, he had to face the fact that this team was a little dysfunctional. But he recognized that perhaps there was an opportunity to upgrade his Bad Work and turn part of it—the task of making this team effective—into Good or even Great Work.

▶ Likewise, there was an opportunity to do more Great Work in other parts of the business. When he asked himself, *How could my role in creating cooperation within the team and across these different groups be Great Work?* ideas for new approaches and things he could do started to bubble up.

Even though this exercise simply paints a picture of how things are now, it can open the door to new insights as to where more Great Work might lie.

BEYOND THE MAP

Completing this exercise gives you an intuitive snapshot of your mix of Bad, Good, and Great Work. Here are two other ways you can deepen your understanding: first, by better quantifying what your mix actually is, and second, by imagining what your perfect mix might be.

Look back: Check your calendar and diary from the last week or so to review how much time you actually spent on Bad, Good, and Great Work. Get clearer about how you're really spending your time and what's truly got your focus. Over the next week, keep track of what you do and categorize how you divide your time among the three categories of work. Just as tracking your spending can help you create a budget, tracking how you spend your time can help you find ways to do more Great Work.

> Life is the sum of all your choices.
>
> *ALBERT CAMUS*

Look forward: What do you think the best mix is for you right now? How much Great Work? How much Good Work? (I hope there's no Bad Work.) If you could have that ideal combination, what would you be doing differently? What would you be doing the same? What would you have to stop? What would you have to start?

Here's a somewhat extreme example that combines looking both back and forward: Jim Collins, the author of *From Good to Great,* uses a stopwatch with three separate timers to time everything he does. He's figured out what his ideal Great Work mix is—his goal is to spend 50 percent of his time on creative work, 30 percent teaching, and 20 percent on the rest.

DEBRIEFING THE MAP

Doing the exercise is a good thing, but the real learning comes when you give yourself a minute or two to do a quick self-debriefing about what just happened and what you learned. To help you recognize and remember your insights from this exercise, answer these questions:

▶ What's the main thing you noticed from this exercise? What's the one key Aha! you've had about your Bad, Good, and Great Work mix?

▶ What, if anything, surprised you? Was it the amount of Bad Work?—and what tasks fell into that category? Was it how much Good Work you're doing? Was it something to do with your Great Work?

▶ What are the habits and patterns that got you to this current mix? What have you been saying yes to that you wish you'd been saying no to?

▶ What do you know now that you didn't know before?

▶ What do you want to remember from this exercise?

Great Work Wisdom

TOWARD ABUNDANCE

BY DAVE AND WENDY ULRICH

In today's complex world, simply being willing and able to do one's work is not enough. We need to find meaning in the work we do. This involves finding work that offers purpose, fulfillment, contribution, connection, and hope. Of course we find meaning in many settings—in the privacy of our homes and the expanses of nature, in churches, ballparks, and community centers, in our relationships with family and friends. But many of us spend the majority of our waking hours at work. So it is vital that we find ways to make the organizations where we work more meaningful and abundant.

We define an abundant organization as *a work setting in which individuals coordinate their aspirations and actions to create meaning for themselves, value for stakeholders, and hope for humanity at large.* As we explored the concept of an abundant organization, we identified eight questions that individuals may ask themselves and leaders may ask their organizations, questions that can help reveal and make more accessible meaning and abundance.

1. **WHAT AM I KNOWN FOR? (IDENTITY)** A sense of abundance is fostered by a clear sense of who we are, what we believe in, and what we are good at. This question probes our character strengths and personal values and how they form the reputation by which we are known.

   Abundant organizations build on strengths and abilities that strengthen others.

2. **WHERE AM I GOING? (PURPOSE AND DIRECTION)** Abundance emerges from a clear sense of what we are trying to accomplish and why. When our personal goals align with the organization's goals, work feels like a meaningful extension of our ▶

private journey. When we both internalize and personalize our company's mission, we find opportunities to impact broad societal problems we care about.

Abundant organizations sustain both fiscal and social responsibility.

3. WHOM DO I TRAVEL WITH? (TEAMWORK) Our sense of abundance is enhanced by meaningful relationships. The increasing complexities of today's workplaces require increasing cooperation and teamwork of many kinds for success. Our meaningful work relationships include friendships, mentoring relationships, and professional networks.

Abundant organizations take work relationships beyond high-performing teams to high-relating teams.

4. WHAT CHALLENGES INTEREST ME? (ENGAGEMENT) The most engaged employees are generally those whose work gives them the opportunity to stretch while doing work they love. Different people find different kinds of work easy, energizing, and enjoyable, and different types of problems meaningful.

Abundance occurs when companies can engage not only employees' skills (competence) and loyalty (commitment), but also their values (contribution).

5. HOW DO I BUILD A POSITIVE WORK ENVIRONMENT? (EFFECTIVE CONNECTION)
While bad habits thrive on isolation and shame, positive routines keep us grounded in what matters most and help us connect with ourselves and others. Organizations can have cynical, negative, demeaning cultures, or they can encourage constructive, affirming, uplifting cultures that help create abundance.

Abundant organizations create positive work environments that affirm and connect people throughout the organization.

6. HOW DO I RESPOND TO SETBACKS? (RESILIENCE AND LEARNING) Failure can be a powerful impetus to growth and learning. When we take risks to work outside our comfort zones, resist defensiveness about mistakes, learn from failure, and keep trying, we become not only more resilient, but more satisfied with life. Abundance is less about getting things right and more about moving in the right direction.

Abundant organizations use principles of resilience and learning to persevere with both people and products.

7. WHAT DELIGHTS ME? (CIVILITY AND DELIGHT) Abundance thrives on simple pleasures. Sources of delight might include laughing at ourselves, appreciating excellence, relishing beauty, being present in the moment, and having fun at work.

Abundant organizations not only attend to outward demographic diversity but also to the diversity of what makes individuals feel happy, cared for, and excited about life.

8. HOW DO I MANAGE THE TRANSITIONS NECESSITATED BY CHANGE? (ENABLING TRANSITION) Abundance can be either threatened or enhanced by changes in the air. In a world of almost constant change, organizations must adapt or fall by the wayside, yet most individuals don't really like constant upheaval and disruption. While change can make us anxious, in the space between the old and the new, both creativity and freshness can also proliferate.

Abundant organizations help individuals internalize the behavioral, cognitive, and affective transitions necessitated by change.

When abundance replaces deficit thinking and action, individuals gain by finding meaning, and organizations gain by increasing productivity, customer share, and investor confidence. ■

Dave Ulrich *has been ranked the No. 1 Management Educator & Guru by* BusinessWeek. *He has written fifteen books covering topics in HR and leadership and is a professor at the Ross School of Business, University of Michigan, and cofounder of the RBL Group (www.rbl.net).*

Wendy Ulrich, PhD, *is the author of* Forgiving Ourselves: Getting Back Up When We Let Ourselves Down, *published by Deseret Book and the founder of Sixteen Stones Center for Growth in Alpine, Utah.*

PART 2

Seeds of Your Great Work

It's Time to Get Going

You've now got a sense of just what is Bad, Good, and Great Work for you. And you've got a sense of your current mix, just how much of each kind of work is showing up in your life right now.

If you're happy with that mix, then we can all relax and you can put the book down and carry on with things. Mazel tov! But if you're not completely satisfied, if you want to make a change, and in particular if you want to do more Great Work, it's time to get going.

The starting point for doing more Great Work is to get clearer on who you are, what you stand for, and what matters to you. These next three maps can help you do that.

In Map 2, you'll look at peak moments from your past and see how they can point you to peak moments in your future. In Map 3, you'll find a new way to articulate how you are when you're at your best and what you're like when you're not at your best. And in the final map of this section, Map 4, you'll see how your heroes and role models can provide great insight as to what qualities you might seek to embody in your own Great Work.

MAP 2

What's Great?

Your past holds clues to your future Great Work

THIS IS NOT AN "INVESTMENT OPPORTUNITY." Have you seen those advertisements for mutual funds that promise wonderful results, and then say in small print that "past performance is no indicator of future results"? Well, that's *not* true when it comes to Great Work. Past performance—or more specifically, past moments of engagement and meaning—is actually a very good indicator of future results. Clues to what Great Work is for you are preserved—like insects in amber—in the peak moments of your past.

WHAT EXACTLY IS A PEAK MOMENT?

A peak moment is a time when you could see and feel yourself doing something more than what you typically do, when you stepped beyond where you normally stay and did something new, tried something different, and made an impact. It's a time when you felt fulfilled and present in your job, when you felt most like yourself.

How our peak moments look and feel is unique to each of us. That's one of the paradoxes and complexities of Great Work.

A peak moment can be like that scene in the movie *Titanic* when Leonardo DiCaprio leans into the wind and yells, "I'm the king of the world!" It can be like that intense fist pump that Roger Federer does when he wins a point. It can be like that look on the face of a gymnast when she "sticks" a landing in the Olympics.

It can be a quiet certainty that your contribution to the meeting was the one that tipped the balance and made it click. It can be the moment when you finally untangle a challenge that you've been trying to figure out for a long time. It can be the time when the work you've done on a project that's excited you and kept you involved and engaged and at your best for the last few months finally comes to fruition—the culmination of a project, the moment when you press a literal or metaphorical "go" switch and it (whatever it is) starts.

It can be an hour when you rise to a challenge and sort out a crisis that's causing disruption in your workplace. It can be when you have a sudden moment of realization, almost as if you're floating outside of yourself—*Wow, I'm doing this and I'm doing it well and I'm thrilled to be doing it.*

It can be about a big, public project or a small, private triumph. But whatever the context, it is a moment of certainty, a moment of insight when you say to yourself, *Yes, this is something to remember. This is me at my most essential, most authentic, and best.*

> Celebrate what you want to see more of.
>
> TOM PETERS

31

MAP 2: WHAT'S GREAT?

THE POWER OF THE PEAK MOMENT

One of the beauties of stopping to acknowledge your peak moments is that they can help you clarify your personal definition of success.

Rather than asking yourself, *Did I do it well? Was I praised? Did I get recognition and a pat on the back? Did I win the prize?* you ask, *Did this have meaning for me? Did this stretch me, teach me, make me happy?*

Doing this exercise helps expand the options before us. We often limit what we can and should do by our education, our training, our work history. For instance, if you are a lawyer, you probably define your skills and capabilities in terms of being a lawyer and doing lawyerlike things.

Peak moments get us beyond that. They tap the power of subjective experience rather than objective accomplishments. When you think about your peak moments (as you are about to do), remember, recall how you *felt,* not what you outwardly accomplished (although the two can go hand in hand).

COMPLETING THE MAP

1. **Think back and remember three or four peak moments over the course of your working life.** For some people, this will be a cinch—they'll instantly be able to point to various moments when they felt they were at their best. For most of us, it won't be so immediate. We might go blank, think, *I've never had a single great moment in my entire working career,* or we might just feel confused and a little overwhelmed.

   Don't panic. It might be worth rereading the "Six Great Work Paradoxes" on pages 11–13 to remind yourself that Great Work is different for each of us.

   Take your time and, with your mind's eye, scan your memory and zero in on the times you were doing meaningful work, work that brought out your best self. It's likely that you knew at the time that this was something significant. It's something you're proud of, something that has stayed in your memory and perhaps even now brings a smile to your face and a thrill to your heart as you remember what you did.

2. **If you wish, add one or two peak moments from outside your work life.** You might choose something from time with friends or family, volunteer work, home improvement, playing a sport, or enjoying a hobby. (Parents, I'm going to ask you not to count the birth of your children. I know it's a peak moment, but for the sake of the exercise, I'd like you to focus on a moment that was all about you.)

3. **Give each one of those peak moments a title, and write down the title in the triangles on the map.**

4. **Now write a short description (one or two sentences) of what happened.** You might consider asking such questions as:

> The most exciting phrase to hear in science, the one that heralds the new discoveries, is not "Eureka!" (I found it) but "That's funny...."
>
> *ISAAC ASIMOV*

- ▶ How were you "at your best" (or near to it) in this situation?
- ▶ How did you feel?
- ▶ Where did it occur?
- ▶ What was your role?
- ▶ What did you do? What behaviors did you exhibit?
- ▶ What didn't you do? What behaviors weren't you exhibiting?
- ▶ What skills did you use?
- ▶ How did you overcome any difficulties?
- ▶ What was the key moment that made the difference?

> ► Who else was involved, if anyone?
> ► What are you particularly proud of?

5. **Now look along the row of these peak-moment stories.** Do you see any emerging themes, any similarities throughout? For instance, are you collaborating or alone? Is there a particular behavior that recurs? Is there a role you seem to favor? These themes are clues as to where the seeds of your Great Work lie. Some of the themes will be about you—what you're like and what you're doing when you're connected to Great Work. Some will be about the types of situations that tend to help you do more Great Work.

GETTING INSIGHTS FROM THE MAP

1. **As you remember those peak moments, what did they feel like for you?** Just sit for a moment, take three slow breaths, and get those feelings "in your bones." Remembering what it feels like to do Great Work, getting a clear sense of it in your body, is useful. It can be a powerful "internal compass" to help you know whether you are or are not doing Great Work.

2. **Take your list of themes and discuss it with someone who knows you well—a spouse, a close friend, a longtime colleague.** Ask them what they think, if this is a good reflection of you at your best. Ask them what's missing. Ask them if they'd use any different words.

3. **The peak moment can be the culminating "Aha!" of a situation.** Retrace the steps you took that got you there. How did it all begin? What decisions did you make? How did you get into the place where the opportunity for Great Work presented itself? What or who else was there then but might be missing now?

FOR EXAMPLE . . .

Sarika's been on the fast track since she joined her consumer goods company, which produces and markets food of various brands for supermarkets. She's recently achieved a milestone promotion, from director to vice president of information technology (IT).

There have been a number of perks to the promotion, including a raise, the status of her new title, her first company car, and some stock options, but for all the benefits, her new role is proving tougher than she thought it would.

Her technical prowess, the reason for her early success, is suddenly not as vital as it once was. Instead, she has to focus more on managing her bigger team and, even more important, on building her influence among her new colleagues at the VP level.

> If you're able to be yourself, then you have no competition. All you have to do is get closer and closer to that essence.
>
> BARBARA COOK

She has a sense that this will be her next Great Work Project, and it's quite a challenge. Although her new boss, the senior VP, is a fan, she has two strikes against her. She is a woman, and all her other colleagues are men. And she is younger than most of her new executive colleagues.

When doing the peak-moment map, the first story Sarika told was of a project she had led the previous year. It involved working with an external vendor to implement a new IT infrastructure for the organization. The project had started badly and quickly gotten worse. In no time, Sarika was under fire from all sides: her boss was anxious, her team was dispirited, and the vendor was now treating them as the enemy rather than as partners. The peak moment had come when she'd called the lead person on the vendor team and set up an "off-site and off-the-record" conversation—a drink after work.

That conversation turned things around. Sarika not only told the vendor exactly what she was looking for but she also talked about her own concerns and owned up to her role in the current situation. From there, the vendor relationship improved dramatically, which went a long way toward reinvigorating her team. She got the project back on track.

Sarika lit up as she told that story. She was very proud to have rectified a bad situation. But when she thought about what was behind the story, she got more reflective. As she wrote out her core behaviors when doing Great Work, this is what she found:

▶ Building relationships and bringing together different parties
▶ Solving crises
▶ Taking the lead
▶ Role-modeling honest conversation

She found similar themes in her other stories. It seemed that whenever she was doing Great Work, she was gathering together disparate people and making them work together, showing people what honest, direct conversation is.

All this was a useful reminder to Sarika. It didn't provide an immediate solution to her current work challenge, but it reminded her what she was best at, and already thoughts were stirring about how she could use these Great Work behaviors to prove herself to her new colleagues.

MY OWN PEAK-MOMENT STORY

Let me tell you a story about a peak moment of my own. In between finishing high school and going to college, I spent a year in England working at a private school. I thought I was going to be a sort of odd-job guy but ended up—even though I'd only just turned eighteen—working full-time as a teacher.

Clearly the school was short-staffed and desperate or just had a moment of madness. Or perhaps both. In any case, I was totally out of my depth.

I was assigned a class of ten-year-old boys. They all had learning difficulties. Six were deaf, four profoundly so. And a bunch of them were hyperactive and found it hard to focus.

In the six months I taught them, only once did I have them all sitting quietly and reading. That was a small moment of glory in itself, but the day that really stands out was when one of the kids had thrown a chair through the window. There was glass, tears, shouting, fighting—in short, a riot.

From any objective perspective, this was not going well. But internally, for me this was shaping up to be a peak moment. Even in the midst of this chaos, there was something compelling about what was going on and about what I needed to do to sort it out—although at the moment I probably couldn't have articulated what the compelling thing was.

Winning back control and the trust of that group became Great Work for me. It called on me to stretch myself, to do things I'd not done before, to tap into who I was at my best, and to rise to the occasion. Separating the kids who were fighting, cleaning up the broken glass, and calming the group by staying in control—and by not freaking out myself—all contributed to dealing with the situation.

Now when I interpret my "Help! I'm a teacher!" peak-moment story and some others from my past, I notice these as themes:

ABOUT ME:
- ▸ I'm often teaching or explaining concepts or ideas.
- ▸ I'm often having new ideas and being able to share them.
- ▸ I'm often encouraging people and helping them fulfill their potential.
- ▸ No one is telling me what to do.

ABOUT THE SITUATION:

- ▶ I'm sometimes with people, sometimes not.
- ▶ I like to be trying new things, rather than refining current things.
- ▶ I like opportunities that offer a chance for adventure.
- ▶ I like doing things that are likely to have a big impact.
- ▶ I'm working with a wide range of people.

They are all insights that have guided me toward doing more Great Work. In the same way, you can get useful insights from your own peak moments to provide building blocks for your own Great Work.

BEYOND THE MAP

1. **Ask others to tell their Great-Work stories—your boss, your peers, your team, or your clients.** This isn't a question people are often asked, but in the vast majority of cases, it's one they love to answer. You will hear interesting stories (guaranteed) and they will also give you unparalleled insight into what really matters to the person speaking.

> The scars you acquire while exercising courage will never make you feel inferior.
>
> D. A. BATTISTA

2. **Pick one of the themes that reflects how you behave when you're doing Great Work.** Choose the one that feels most important to you right now and turn your attention to it.

   On a scale of 1 to 10, with 10 being "living it to the fullest" and 1 being "not living it at all," score how you're living that theme right now.

   Now consider this: If you were living that theme 10 out of 10, what would that look like? What would you be doing differently?

DEBRIEFING THE MAP

Take a minute to cement what you learned from the map by answering these questions:

▶ What patterns or commonalities did you notice across your peak moment stories?

▶ What do you think your peak moment stories say about what's important to you?

▶ What did this exercise confirm about your strengths?

▶ What most surprised you in completing this exercise?

▶ What do you know now that you didn't know before?

▶ What was most valuable for you about this exercise?

Great Work Wisdom

A LEAP OF FAITH

BY PENELOPE TRUNK

Most people who are not doing Great Work blame it on their work circumstances. And that's easy enough to do—there's always someone or something you can point the finger at. Too much work, not enough work. The wrong people at the right time, the right people at the wrong time. Goals that are too difficult to attain, goals that are too easy.

But Great Work is internal, and ultimately the choice to find it or not find it is yours. You do not need to get paid to do Great Work. No one can keep you from doing Great Work by giving you a stupid job. You can do Great Work because you're great. Maybe you do it at home, after the office. Maybe you do it in your head, when you go to the bathroom at work. Maybe you do it despite what your "job description" calls for.

Ultimately, you are left with you. So really, doing Great Work is about knowing who you are and what you want. And here's the crux of the matter: We can never know that for sure. You'll never know everything about who you are, and you'll never be able to completely describe what you want.

But we can't wait forever. So we have to guess and take the plunge. Stepping forward to do more Great Work is in fact about a leap of faith that we take because the alternatives are so disappointing. ■

Penelope Trunk *is CEO of Brazen Careerist (www.BrazenCareerist.com), the number-one community for Gen Y to manage their careers. She has been a software executive, founded three companies, and played professional beach volleyball. She has a syndicated column and is the author of* Brazen Careerist: The New Rules for Success.

MAP 3

What Are You Like at Your Best?

What Great and Not So Great look like

WHEN I WORKED IN THE WORLD of innovation and marketing, I'd often find myself trying to explain to a client the essence of a particular brand. It would be a struggle to find the right words that would explain its nuances, articulate how it stood out from the pack, and describe what type of person it would appeal to.

We all have the extraordinary coded within us, waiting to be released.

DR. JEAN HOUSTON

For instance, how is one high-end vodka different from another? There's really not much difference between them, after all. Close your eyes, and do a blind test and they all pretty much taste like vodka. So how do you pin down whatever difference there might be?

The answer is to use metaphor to add color and depth to the picture you're painting.

A METAPHOR IS WORTH A THOUSAND PICTURES

What makes this exercise really powerful is to pair metaphors, so you get a sense of both what the subject is and what it is not. That comparison helps refine what you mean, making it more specific and more useful.

So rather than trying to find the words to describe vodka (clear, strong, alcoholic), I might articulate a particular brand's feel and essence by saying it is:

- ▶ Expensive denim, *not* Leather
- ▶ Mediterranean, *not* Scandinavian
- ▶ Classical, *not* Baroque
- ▶ Pomegranate, *not* Green apple
- ▶ Bold, *not* Pastel
- ▶ The 1960s, *not* The 1990s
- ▶ A couple talking, *not* A group dancing

And so on, all to try to pin down how the "vibe" of this vodka is different from all the other high-end vodkas. (For some reason, I've got this strong urge to drink a martini.)

FROM BRANDING TO BEING

When I moved out of innovation and marketing into personal development and executive coaching, I immediately saw how the same approach could be used to help reveal who you were at your best. The same principles apply—what's the yes *and* what's the no—but they are focused on your behavior and attitude, rather than whether you should end up on the top shelf of an expensive bar or not. Gaining insight into who you are—and who you are not—is a powerful act.

MAP 3: WHAT ARE YOU LIKE AT YOUR BEST?

I am this...   ...not that

Map 3: What Are You Like at Your Best?

1. **Remember a time when you were at your very best.** It will be a time when you felt you were being most authentic, most yourself, most natural, most "in the zone." It might be one of the peak moments you described in the previous exercise. Or it might be another time, a time when you were playing to your strengths or doing Great Work. Bring it into your mind's eye now.

2. **Write down twenty words that evoke how you were at this time.** They can describe how you were feeling or thinking (for example, joyful, excited, creative, powerful, ambitious) or how you were behaving (for example, not taking it too seriously, taking charge). Don't censor yourself—just jot down any words that come to mind. You'll have a chance to edit later. (And yes, I know twenty words is a lot. I'm pushing you here.)

3. **Think of another time when you were similarly rocking along, another moment when you felt you were at your best and most yourself.** Add another ten words to your list. Some will be variations on the twenty you already have (and that's fine), but try also to find some new words.

4. **Now narrow that list down to the ten words that seem the most powerful and on-target to you.** They should be the ten that seem to best sum you up when you're in the flow, when you're having the most impact, when you're being how you want to be.

5. **See if you can amp up your words.** Grab a thesaurus (or go online to www.visualthesaurus.com) and see if there's a slightly better version of any of the words you've already got. Play around to see if you can tweak your words to make them even more accurate and useful for you. You want to have a word or phrase that really resonates with you.

6. **Decide upon your final (for now) list of ten words and write them down in the left-hand column.** This is your "When I'm at my best, I am this" column.

7. **Now it's time for the second part of the exercise.** We're going to complete the other column, the ". . . not that" column. You're looking for the words or metaphors that capture what you're like when you're falling a little short of the peak-moment state.

8. **Pick one word in the left-hand column you've already completed.** Now find a word that describes the safe, default, OK-but-not-great behavior that you recognize to be true about yourself when you're not at your best. The word won't necessarily be the literal or extreme opposite of the partner word in the left-hand column. So the partner to "joyful" might not be "depressed" but "ho-hum." The partner to "calm" might not be "manic" but "agitated." The secret to making this column work for you is to have words that describe behaviors you know to be true about you.

9. **Just as you did with the words in the first column, play around and tweak these words.** The goal is to find the most powerful, most accurate way to describe your state of being when you're not at your best.

GETTING INSIGHTS FROM THE MAP

I. **There are two routes to doing more Great Work.** One is to figure out where the opportunities might be and then start to take them on. (Nothing at all wrong with that, by the way—that's what Maps 5 to 7 are all about.) And another is to figure out how you behave when you're doing Great Work and start to behave like that as often as possible—then see what Great Work starts to blossom. This second way may seem slightly counterintuitive, but it can work just as well as the first—and sometimes it is the easier place to begin.

2. **If you're feeling that you're not quite being your best self now, that you're somehow running a little slow, scan the right-hand column.** Which of those words capture how you are now? And what are the words paired with them in the left-hand column? For instance, you might notice that you're "playing it safe." Your paired phrase might be "being provocative." How then can you shift your behavior to move closer to that standard?

FOR EXAMPLE . . .

Only a couple of years earlier, Janet had been a student, finishing her degree and looking forward to working, earning a salary, and beginning her career.

Now she was twenty-six, putting in long hours as a corporate lawyer and wondering what it was really all about. Those first months had been intense, bewildering, exciting, and very, very busy. She worked six days a week to keep up with her cases and other responsibilities, as well as learning to navigate the politics of her firm.

Finally she was getting a chance to take a breath. She'd just earned her first promotion, and it was an opportunity to pause and see if there was more to her career than just working hard.

In completing Map 3, she had a chance to remember what she was like when she was at her best and take stock of what she was like when she was at less than her best. As she scanned the previous years of work and thought back to what she was like at college, she generated this list:

We are all worms, but I do believe I'm a glowworm.

WINSTON CHURCHILL

AT MY BEST, I'M THIS, *NOT* THAT:

- ▶ Keeping my sense of humor, *not* Feeling it's all very serious
- ▶ Changing the world, *not* Thinking only business matters
- ▶ Joyful, *not* Dour
- ▶ Working in groups, *not* Working solo
- ▶ Seeing the big picture, *not* Dealing with minutiae
- ▶ Creating options, *not* Following the rules
- ▶ Dealing with people, *not* Isolated and working alone
- ▶ Connected and networking, *not* Hiding and staying small
- ▶ In the spotlight, *not* In the wings

It was a sobering list for Janet. The truth was, when she looked back over her experience at the law firm, she found she spent most of her time in the ". . . not that" column and not nearly enough time in the "this" column. Things weren't totally hopeless; it wasn't as if she *never* did work that was engaging and meaningful, but the percentage of Great Work was much too low and that of Bad Work was much too high.

Janet's promotion presented a perfect time to reflect on what she wanted to be different in her work life. She knew she had an opportunity to make a change, and had some hard thinking to do about how she might bring more Great Work into her new role.

BEYOND THE MAP

I. **Once you have a set of words that works for you, consider putting it somewhere you can see it every day.** I have one copy on my bulletin board near my desk, and I've had another one laminated to take with me when I'm going to give a talk or run a workshop.

2. **Pick one of the word pairs and give it your attention for a day or a week.** You might choose a word in the left column and tell yourself, *Today, I'm going to be as fully X as I can.* Or you might pick a word from the right column and say to yourself, *Today, I'm going to watch out for every time I default to this behavior, and when I notice that, I'm going to shift to something different.*

3. **Keep working with your list.** I've found you can quickly get it to about 80 percent right—pairs of words that do a pretty good job of capturing a useful this/not that dichotomy—but occasionally revisiting and tweaking the words can help make this list even more focused and useful.

DEBRIEFING THE MAP

Internalize what you've learned from this map by answering the following questions:

▶ What's the main thing you noticed from this exercise?

▶ When you scan the words in the left-hand column, what do you feel? What do you think? What does that tell you?

▶ When you scan the words in the right-hand column, what do you feel? What do you think? What does that tell you?

▶ What do you know now about yourself that you hadn't fully realized before?

▶ What's an action you can take now (or soon) as a result of completing this exercise?

MAP 4

Who's Great?

Tap the power of role models

I'VE DONE PLENTY OF HERO WORSHIPPING in my time. Just to name a few, I've revered:

- ► My dad, who always takes the high ground with a quiet integrity
- ► My classmate Phil, who at the age of four could color inside the lines and got the gold star from Mrs. Wright, our teacher
- ► Alex Jesaulenko, the star of the Carlton Football Club, my favorite team.

In the early days, this hero worship was a mixture of awe and jealousy. I was envious of what they could do and unhappily certain I couldn't do it myself. But over time, things have shifted to a more subtle appreciation of my role models.

I'm beginning to see the people I admire as a call to me to be my best, encouraging and pulling me forward to the same standard of whatever it is that they embody.

THE BEING AND THE DOING

That's particularly true these days, when I connect with who my heroes *are*, not just what they *do*—their characteristics rather than their achievements. That's why Dad is still a hero (his integrity is part of his being), whereas Phil's ability to color accurately is no longer quite such a big deal.

Focusing on the being rather than the doing also prevents us from giving up, knowing we could never equal the performance. I'll never play tennis like Rafael Nadal, but I can strive to emulate his tenacity, his refusal to give up. I expect and hope I'll never be persecuted like Nelson Mandela, but I can try to embody some of his graciousness and ability to forgive.

HEROES ARE ALL AROUND US

The other thing to know here is that heroes are all around us. You don't have to draw only from the sporting pantheon, *Entertainment Tonight,* and mythological or historical leaders. Your hero and role model may be a teacher, a neighbor, a colleague, or a friend. In fact, you can look at almost anyone and ask, *What is it about this person that I most admire? What's best about who they are?*

COMPLETING THE MAP

1. **Think of eight heroes, role models you think are inspiring for one reason or other.** They can be famous or not (George Clooney, your mother), real or not (Queen Elizabeth, Buzz Lightyear), alive or not (Desmond Tutu, Gandhi). Scan your world, and think about people whose stories capture your imagination, folks you've always held in high esteem, who embody something you think is impressive—You might even be a bit envious of them. (I know, eight is a lot. But stick with it.)

MAP 4: WHO'S GREAT?

1.

2.

3.

4.

1.

2.

3.

4.

1.

2.

3.

4.

1.

2.

3.

4.

1.

2.

3.

4.

DOWNLOAD A FREE TEMPLATE OF THIS MAP
AT WWW.DOMOREGREATWORK.COM.

2. **The role models don't even have to be people.** If it resonates with you, a hero could be an object that you admire or that sparks your imagination (for example, the Mini Cooper or a Ford truck) or even a company or organization that you think does great work (for example, Apple or Greenpeace or Google).

3. **Narrow that list to five.** Chose the five you feel are most compelling, about whom you'd be most likely to say, *Yes, I'd like to embody what they've got,* and put a name at the top of each of the circles.

4. **For each hero, list four of the characteristics that are so inspiring to you.** These can be behaviors exhibited, qualities you sense, or situations he, she, or it has created.

GETTING INSIGHTS FROM THE MAP

There are a number of ways you can use this map:

1. **Look for patterns in your lineup of role models.** Recurring themes or words can give you a clue about what you believe is important, how you'd like to behave, and where seeds of your own Great Work might lie. For example, if variations on a theme of creativity keep recurring in the description of your heroes, that's a big clue that your Great Work will involve and engage your own creativity.

2. **When you're feeling discombobulated and unsure of your next move, bring one of your role models to mind and ask:**
   ▶ How would [insert hero's name] behave right now?
   ▶ What would [insert hero's name] do?

Doing that might help you get out of your current mind-set and reveal alternative ways to approach the situation at hand.

FOR EXAMPLE . . .

We met Sarika doing Map 2 as she started to think about her Great Work Project—how to have more impact and influence in her new role as VP of IT.

In working through this map, she deliberately chose role models from different parts of her life—people from work and her life outside work, as well as people she didn't know personally but liked for what they stood for.

When she whittled down her list, she had the names of five heroes and characteristics she admired about each one:

- **Her former boss, Jason:** challenging, willing to trust people and give them a chance, brilliant at managing upward and keeping his boss happy, always thinks about the big picture.

- **Her friend Mary:** sparky, not afraid to be the center of attention, always full of ideas (some good, some a little crazy), has a great network, and is willing to use it.

- **Annie Lennox of the Eurythmics:** stylish, works well solo and in partnership, strong, creative.

- **Indiana Jones:** courageous, has adventures, has a sense of humor, willing to challenge the baddies, stops at nothing to achieve his goal.

- **Craig Newmark, founder of Craigslist:** does work that makes a difference to the world, brilliant at bringing together the right people, willing to use technology in creative ways.

Reviewing the list, Sarika already felt there was something valuable there, as if she'd created her own board of advisors that she could turn to for mentoring.

When she considered the role models as a group, she noticed two themes in particular:

▶ Sparky, creative, uses technology creatively

▶ Manages upward, creates and uses a network, works in partnership

Sarika started to realize a simple but powerful truth: If she could increase the extent to which she was creative and/or working in partnership, she would most likely also do more Great Work. She didn't yet have to know how or where she was going to be creative or find opportunities for partnership; she'd get to that in time (and as she kept working through the book). But knowing these were clues to success lifted her spirits. It was also interesting (and reassuring) to see how themes that emerged when she pinpointed her peak moments from the previous map were coming up again in this exercise.

> We need role models who are going to break the mold.
>
> *CARLY SIMON*

BEYOND THE MAP

1. **Know that you are a role model to others.** It's not as though you're a blank slate—you've got a number of essential characteristics that are ready to be harnessed for Great Work. But sometimes it's hard to see yourself clearly. So imagine that your friends and peers are discussing your best characteristics, what they love most about you, what makes you the unique person you are. What characteristics do you think they would list? See if you can come up with five—and this is no time for bashfulness or false modesty.

2. **Turn up the volume! Choose a characteristic that one of your heroes embodies.** Now think about how it's currently showing up in your life. If you

had a volume knob connected to it, what would it be set at now? What would you look like, sound like, and be like if it was turned up to the maximum volume?

> When I was a kid I never learned to play. I actually got in bands through watching people play and copying them.
>
> *CHARLIE WATTS*

3. Build a picture montage of role models. Cut out pictures from magazines or find them on the Internet. Paste them on a sheet of paper or pin them to a bulletin board, and keep the montage somewhere you'll see it regularly. For those of us who respond best to visual information, this is a great way of staying connected to the Great Work attributes that your heroes embody and that you'd like to see in yourself.

DEBRIEFING THE MAP

Expand and cement the insights offered by the map by answering the following questions:

▶ What was most powerful about listing your heroes?

▶ Who surprised you by showing up on your list? What surprised you?

▶ What characteristic showed up that you have and that you take for granted?

▶ What's become clearer about who you are and who you want to be?

Understand Your Motivation

If you want to do more Great Work, you're asking yourself to make a change. But even as you read this, perhaps fired up by the new possibilities that you're starting to imagine, part of you remembers that you (like all of us) have a spotty track record with change.

Think about your New Year's resolutions from the years past. How many were still alive and strong in mid-February? If you're like most of us, not many. In fact, the third Monday of January has been termed the most depressing day of the year. It's when our credit card bills are due *and* our resolutions finally crumble.

Think of your attempts to lose weight. A few months after beginning a diet, most of us are the same weight we were before—and perhaps a little heavier.

Think of the guidance you've received in your annual performance review. You know that at least some of it was fair and valid, but even with your best intention to change, the following year you got much the same feedback.

> You can't wait for inspiration. You have to go after it with a club.
>
> *JACK LONDON*

Bottom line? It's often very difficult to change your behavior. But it can get a little easier if you understand two influences on that behavior that are often largely unconscious—our unspoken ▶

57

commitments and our motivation patterns.

YOUR UNSPOKEN COMMITMENTS

Robert Kegan and Lisa Laskow Lahey speak of our "immunity to change" in their book of the same title. Their powerful insight is that while we might want to behave differently (for example, be more assertive in meetings) in order to achieve a new goal (be more influential in the team), the way we're behaving right now (being quiet and passive in meetings) serves another, deeper, and often unspoken goal or commitment (for instance, being seen as a team player, being liked, or building a reputation as a noncomplainer).

This insight can cause a flash of the blindingly obvious. Of course! That's why I don't do action X, even though I profess to want to do it. I'm too deeply committed to continuing to do action Y, and that's what's preventing me from doing something different.

In other words, before you focus on doing more Great Work, it is useful to step back and get clear on what's motivating your current behaviors that gets in the way of doing more Great Work. Getting to the heart of your current commitments can be a profound starting point for understanding what might motivate you to do more Great Work—and what might need to change.

MOVING TOWARD, MOVING AWAY

Toward or away from—each of us has a different driver of intrinsic motivation.

Some of us are motivated primarily by what we might *gain* from a situation. We're goal driven, pulled toward opportunities and an outcome.

This "toward" motivation is often about external rewards—money, success, fame, material possessions. But it can also be about internal rewards, such as honoring your values, having the impact you want in the world, rising to a challenge, or gaining control over a situation.

Some of us, on the other hand, are motivated by what we will *avoid* if we achieve our goals. Again, that can be externally driven (not being told off by your boss, not disappointing the team) or it can be internally driven (not stepping on your values, not breaking a promise).

> You don't have to be a fantastic hero to do certain things; to compete. You can be just an ordinary person, sufficiently motivated to reach challenging goals. The intense effort, the giving of everything you've got, is a very pleasant bonus.
>
> *EDMUND HILLARY*

For instance, when my wife and I think about going out to dinner, I'm driven by a "toward" motivation, whereas she's driven by an "away from" motivation. I want a nice meal, but I most want to go somewhere new and different because I'm motivated to have a new experience and try new foods. She wants a nice meal, too, but she most wants to avoid a mediocre (or worse) experience and for that reason tends to want to return to familiar and trusted restaurants. (Sometimes we make it out the door. And sometimes we just end up cooking dinner at home.)

THE BOTTOM LINE

It doesn't really matter which type you are. What can be useful is knowing where you get your drive to do more Great Work. If you're a "toward" sort of person, then you can use that knowledge to actively define goals that will pull you toward Great Work. If you know you're an "away from" type, then you can figure out exactly what you need to manage and avoid in your quest for Great Work. ■

Standing for Something

WHEN YOU ANSWER THE CLARION CALL, "Do More Great Work!" the natural temptation is to scan the field looking for opportunities. *Where's the Great Work? How can I start?* These are good questions, and we are going to explore them in the next section. But we've started not by looking outward, but by looking inward.

You've pinpointed peak moments in Map 2: What's Great? and recognized that these are the feelings that you're looking for in your Great Work. In Map 3: What Are You Like at Your Best? you've examined a range of your behaviors between ho-hum and extraordinary, paving the way to find work that brings out the best in you. And in Map 4: Who's Great? you've articulated the characteristics you admire and would like to embody; your Great Work will tap into those qualities.

SQUARE PEG

When I was very young, I had a simple wooden toy that required me to match objects of various shapes to the appropriate hole in the board. Square peg in the square hole, round peg in the round hole—you know the drill.

The exercises you've completed can play a similar role, both in helping you figure out what your "shape" is and then in finding the best space in which you might fit. For example, Sarika's shape is influenced by her need to be creative, to collaborate, and to solve problems. Knowing your own shape will help you to find the space that fits you best.

First, it will make it clearer faster when you're the proverbial square peg in a round hole. In Janet's story, you see her becoming more aware of what is and what is not working in her role at the law firm. Becoming more sensitive to what's not a fit makes these situations less tolerable—and makes it more likely that you'll change something to do more Great Work.

Second, knowing your shape will help you recognize when you've found a good fit—when who you are and what matters to you match up with opportunities to do more Great Work.

In the next section of the book, the insights you've gained by looking at yourself and at the landscape around you will pave the way for the following exercises to be more focused and relevant.

PART 3

Uncovering Your Great Work

Matching Lock and Key

At one conference I attended, half the participants were given a closed padlock and the other half were given a key. The test: to find your partner and open the lock.

It was a fun way to meet people and provided a starting point for conversation beyond the weather, sports, and the commute. And it provides a great metaphor for where you are right now.

You've got a key—a sense of who you are, what you stand for, what matters to you. Now you're looking for something to unlock. To find and do more Great Work you must shift focus and begin to look more expansively at what surrounds you.

In Map 5 you'll scan your world and workplace for openings, possibilities, and opportunities that might be calling you to do more Great Work.

In Map 6 you'll tap into what's "broken" in your work life and uncover places where your Great Work might be to right something that's wrong.

And in Map 7 you'll drill down into your obligations in your workplace and see how you can balance what you want to do with what your organization requires you to do.

MAP 5

What's Calling You?

Scan your life for Great Work opportunities

LAST SUMMER, I SPENT A WEEK hiking near Gros Morne National Park in Newfoundland, one of the most beautiful parts of Canada.

On the first day—with me at my urban, unfit, flabby worst—we spent the morning hours climbing several thousand feet from the shore of a fjord up a mountain spur. It was six long hours of relentless striving, pushing our way through the dense vegetation along a barely marked trail, hauling a heavy pack up what seemed like an endless slope.

Finally we broke clear of the scrub and came out onto Indian Lookout. Below us stretched a necklace of silver lakes strung across the landscape, and in the distance the Gulf of St. Lawrence.

The busyness of our lives can often be like that initial climb. Our attention is on where next to put our foot, how to get through that looming piece of scrub, how to make it to the next rest point.

But to get a sense of where there might be opportunities for Great Work, you need to find a place where you can stop, scan the landscape, and see what might be worth pursuing. You need to get to the lookout.

COMPLETING THE MAP

1. **There are two maps for you to choose from here.** The first, on page 68, is a more general one of opportunities for Great Work in the full landscape of your life. The second, on page 70, is more specific to potential opportunities at work. Pick the map you want to work with now. (You can always come back and tackle the other one later.)

2. **Scan the map you've chosen.** You'll see that it contains areas where there might be opportunities to do more Great Work. The inner ring contains general areas; the outer ring, more specific possibilities.

3. **If it's useful, add details that will customize the map to reflect your life.** For instance, if you're delving into the work map, you could list the current projects you're involved in or list the key relationship you're managing. You can do that either on the map itself, or list them on a separate piece of paper.

4. **You can also customize the map by changing the labels, if you wish—just cross out what's there and replace it with something that works better for you.** Or simply add anything that's missing. You'll see in the life map that there's even a "???" label for you to do just that.

5. **Now that the map is customized to reflect your life, circle five areas where you think there might be opportunities to do more Great Work.** You can circle the more general categories in the inner ring if you wish, but

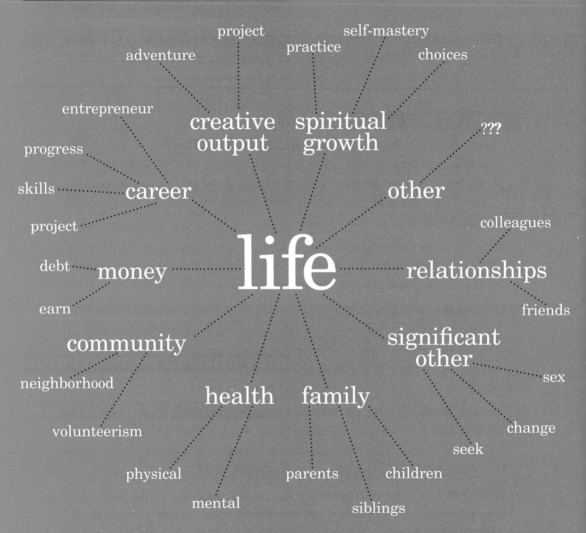

I'd encourage you to spend time on the outer ring, where there are more specific opportunities. In choosing your five areas, you might consider:

▶ Is there an obvious project you've been wanting to do for some time?

▶ What part of the map do you naturally gravitate to?

▶ Where could you enhance the work you're doing, upgrade your effort, and change it from Good to Great?

▶ Where might you begin something new or spark something different?

6. **You'll perhaps want to pick something immediately as your Great Work Project.** Of course, you're welcome to do that. And if you do, congratulations! Just know that the next two maps will give you additional information as to what that project might be, and the following section helps you make the choice. So if you don't know what you want to focus on just yet, that's fine, too.

GETTING INSIGHTS FROM THE MAP

This map helps you get off the trail, with its narrow focus on what's in front of you right now, and up to the lookout point where you can reflect on your whole life for Great Work opportunities.

Scan the map and notice which parts you're immediately drawn to. Those are areas that attract the needle of your internal Great Work compass, which you made more sensitive by the work you did on Maps 2 to 4. It's good to know that sometimes the obvious places are the perfect places to start.

> Everyone should carefully observe which way his heart draws him, and then choose that way with all his strength.
>
> *HASIDIC SAYING*

69

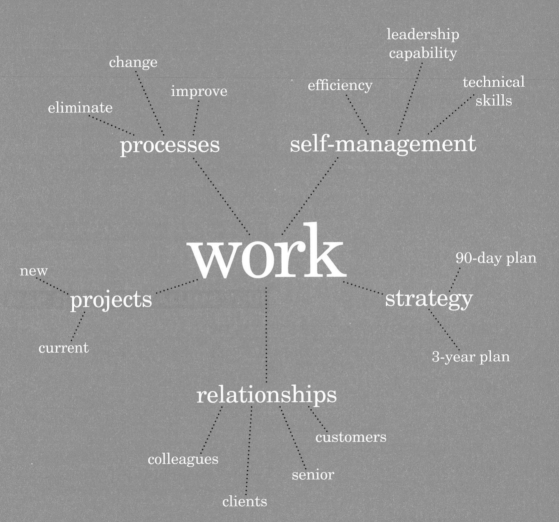

change

improve

eliminate

processes

efficiency

leadership
capability

technical
skills

self-management

work

new

projects

current

strategy

90-day plan

3-year plan

relationships

customers

colleagues

senior

clients

Notice also which parts of the map remind you of the projects you've been wanting to get going on for a while. Perhaps it's time to move them off the "someday/maybe" pile and onto the "I'm going to dig right into this" pile.

Even if you're drawn to certain parts of the map, spend time everywhere. Make sure you've given each nook and cranny of your life the chance to offer an opportunity for Great Work. Ask yourself, *If I* had *to do more Great Work here, what might I do?* Sometimes great things come from the periphery.

> We are not in a position in which we have nothing to work with. We already have capacities, talents, direction, missions, callings.
>
> *ABRAHAM MASLOW*

FOR EXAMPLE . . .

We met Andy doing the first map, when he was taking a snapshot of how things were going as he led his marketing team toward the launch of a product. He found himself with not a whole lot of Great Work and too much Bad Work—much of it created by his dysfunctional team. Even though in the past he had considered creating marketing strategies Great Work, he suspected that now the real Great Work Project for him was getting his team fully functioning.

Andy chose to focus on the work version of Map 5. As he scanned it, three things jumped out as possibilities. He circled relationships/colleagues, self-management/leadership capability and projects/current.

The first possible area involved tackling the issues in his team. When he really thought about it, the crux was getting two members of the team in particular to raise their games and, to put it bluntly, stop their passive resistance to the work.

The second possibility, which he saw was related to the first, was to look at his own leadership role in this team and to raise his own game. As Andy articulated that thought, he realized that this one probably trumped the first challenge. Or rather, if he did this, one of the consequences might be a different level of engagement from some of his team members.

And the final possibility was the product-launch project itself. As Andy thought about that, he concluded that this was the "big picture" Great Work, but the real challenge at the moment was his role in leading the team. Focus on that, and it would have a ripple effect on everything else.

BEYOND THE MAP

Start building a list of possible Great Work Projects. Keep it in a notebook or on your computer or somewhere you can collect opportunities. When you notice opportunities in the ebb and flow of your daily life—things you want to do, things you're frustrated with and want to change, possibilities you've just noticed—jot them down. When the time comes for you to think about what your next Great Work Project might be, you'll have a ready list to draw upon.

DEBRIEFING THE MAP

Recognize and remember your insights by answering these questions:

▶ What did you learn by focusing on the big picture? What surprised you?

▶ What were the obvious opportunities for Great Work that you'd been almost too blind to see?

▶ What might be possible in the less obvious places?

▶ What do you know now about yourself that you hadn't fully realized before?

Great Work Wisdom

THE SECRET TO DOING GREAT WORK

BY SETH GODIN

All this talk about doing Great Work is actually damaging. It encourages you to freeze up, to get stuck, to start believing that you can't possibly do any work that's worthy of the label "great." Along the way, people have brainwashed you into believing that the insightful, inspirational, and nonlinear are reserved for a blessed few. Your gig is mediocre and average, following instructions and fitting in ... the Great Work is for people who somehow deserve it, those who are blessed.

This is nonsense, of course. You've been doing Great Work all your life, but hiding it. You've had brilliant insights or started to make an important difference. Then reality intervenes. You pull back, back off, lighten up. You realize that your Great Work is going to offend or disturb or get you in trouble. What sort of trouble isn't exactly clear, but that's what you've been taught to believe.

My advice for creating Great Work is disarmingly simple: Don't settle.

There are lots of good reasons to settle. You're out of time or money, the boss won't let you. You aren't allowed, or you aren't qualified, or your team will be annoyed.

I'm not saying that there aren't good reasons to settle. Of course there are. But settling is the reason Great Work never sees the light of day. There's nothing left to say, nothing left to read. If you honestly believe that Great Work matters, then the issue is settled. You can and should start today. Identify where you're settling, and stop. ■

Seth Godin *writes the most popular marketing blog in the world (sethgodin.com), and has authored ten bestselling books that have changed the way people think about marketing and work. He has coined many marketing terms, including permission marketing, idea viruses, and purple cows.*

MAP 6

What's Broken?

What pains you can also inspire you

IT'S SUMMER, AND YOU'RE OUTSIDE enjoying a spectacular sunset. As the colors slowly fade, you become aware of a familiar, high-pitched whine. And then the mosquito bites. No problem, you think. It's just a mosquito. I'll stay and enjoy the panorama.

And then another one bites. And then another.

Finally you give up on the view, and beat a retreat indoors.

WHAT'S BITING YOU NOW?

As annoying as they may be, at least with mosquitoes there's a solution at hand. It's harder to get away from the irritants that buzz around us in our daily lives. There's no fast-acting bug spray nearby, no retreat to a screened porch. So we put up with a host of aggravations—some big, some small—that erode the quality of our lives.

Think about your own cloud of metaphorical mosquitoes. What bugs you? What have you been tolerating for a while but want to tolerate no more? What's ho-hum, boring, taken for granted, and could do with a little electroshock therapy?

In short, what's broken and needs to be fixed?

COMPLETING THE MAP

1. **You'll notice that the concentric circles start with what's closest to you and ripple outward to the edge of the universe.** Start in the inner circle and think about what you'd like to change about your desk. (We're starting small, but don't worry. Sometimes a small change can catalyze bigger things, and we'll be expanding the scope fast.)

2. **Work through the circles, and write down at least two things you'd like to change about each of these domains.** Be as specific as you can. The more clearly you can articulate what needs to be different, the more clearly opportunities for Great Work will become apparent.

3. **When you've completed that, go back and circle the five possible candidates for Great Work that you're most drawn to.** Just as with the previous map, you can select:

   ▶ An obvious project you've been wanting to do or a change you've been intending to make for some time

   ▶ An area of natural attraction, something you gravitate toward

   ▶ Something you could enhance, taking it from Bad or Good Work to Great

   ▶ A totally new project, in which you might spark something different

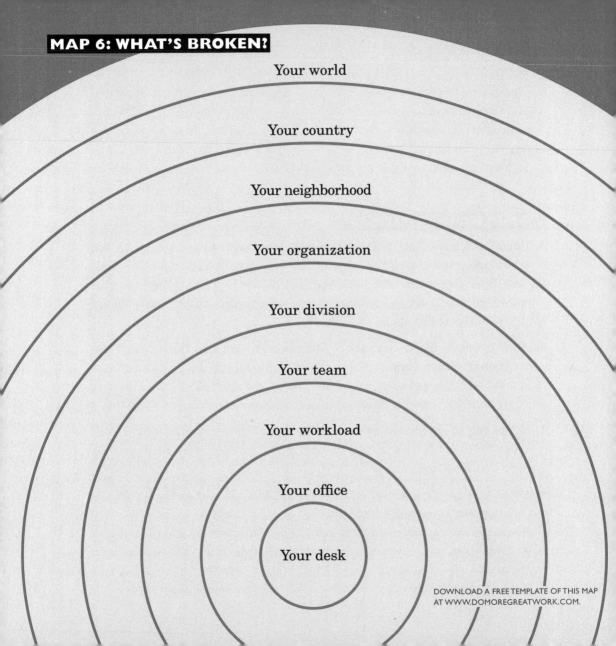

Your world

Your country

Your neighborhood

Your organization

Your division

Your team

Your workload

Your office

Your desk

GETTING INSIGHTS FROM THE MAP

Opportunities for Great Work lurk everywhere, not just in what's going smoothly but also in what's not. Obviously, as you move out through the rings, the scale of what's broken increases—as would the potential impact you'd have if you took on that particular challenge.

To get a sense of where you might start, move your finger up and down the page, noticing how you react to the scale of each challenge.

Some, down near the base of the page, may feel too small to take on as Great Work. (That doesn't mean you shouldn't find time to tidy up these issues.)

Some, as you approach the top of the page, may feel too big to tackle (at least for now).

It's likely that somewhere in the middle there will be some possibilities for Great Work—something broken, a challenge that's the right scale for you to take on.

FOR EXAMPLE . . .

Carlos, a partner in a midsize accounting firm, has felt that things have been going just fine. He enjoys the work and gets along perfectly well with his colleagues—his fellow partners as well as the junior members of the firm.

Recently though, he's begun to be concerned that he's cruising along in Good Work mode and not doing very much Great Work. There's nothing dramatically wrong, but Carlos has the sense that he's on a slippery slope from comfort to routine to rut.

Having completed Maps 2, 3, and 4, Carlos was beginning to get a better idea of who he was when doing Great Work. This was perhaps best captured by the results from Map 3: What Are You Like at Your Best? Here's what he had written down:

Do More Great Work.

AT MY BEST I'M THIS, *NOT* THAT:

- ▶ Sense of fun, *not* Stay serious
- ▶ Exploring options, *not* Doing the most obvious thing
- ▶ Asking questions, *not* "I can do that"
- ▶ New ideas, *not* Obvious solutions
- ▶ Entrepreneurial, *not* "Company man"
- ▶ Deep, *not* Shallow
- ▶ Audi, *not* Mercedes

He wasn't sure exactly what to do with this information just yet. But having a "this is me at my best . . . and not at my best" list was already making him realize that he wasn't playing to his full potential.

Filling out Map 6 provoked a change of outlook for Carlos. Normally, he went on the assumption that "if it's not a crisis, it's fine." Actually looking for what was broken was not something he typically did. The first two circles of Map 6 didn't yield much that excited him. Yes, he could make some tweaks to his desk and office, but it was hardly Great Work. Likewise, the next three circles were interesting but not really stunning. His workload was under control, his team was just fine, judging from a recent internal employee survey and his partners' feedback, and he didn't really have a division.

But things started getting interesting when he thought about what he wanted to change about the firm. In some ways, it occurred to Carlos, the firm was in danger of being in the same rut he was in—moving along just fine, but not really doing much new. Revenue and profit both had hit a plateau. Was the firm stagnating? Suddenly

> I think of a hero as someone who understands the degree of responsibility that comes with his freedom.
>
> *BOB DYLAN*

Carlos started to see a possible connection between what he'd learned about himself and the need for things to change in the firm. In particular, the themes of new ideas, exploring options, and entrepreneurship emerged from his work with Maps 2, 3, and 4.

He wasn't quite sure yet what to do with that thought, but already he was getting excited about the possibility of helping the firm get out of its own rut. One option might be to develop a new service that could change things with their clients and add new revenue. Another option could be to find and close a deal with some new clients.

Carlos moved quickly through the final three circles. The truth was, although there were things in those parts of the map that he'd like to change, it was the organizational ring that had got him hooked.

> There is a crack in everything. That's how the light gets in.
>
> *LEONARD COHEN*

BEYOND THE MAP

Start taking note of the "mosquitoes" in your life, the irritations that you live with every day.

I suspect you'll be amazed at how many there are, some small and some larger. They're like grains of sand in the lubricant of life, and they make everything a little more complicated, a little grittier. Perhaps it's time to address some of these. You can add them to your list of potential Great Work Projects that you're already building from the previous exercise.

Also pay attention to the little things that get in your way but that you put up with. The fact that we tolerate them is even more subtly insidious than the irritants themselves. These are the annoyances we've resigned ourselves to, saying, *I guess I can handle that* or *I can't be bothered to change that right now.* And then often we just stop noticing them and how they dim the light.

Reducing such accepted annoyances one by one is a wonderful way to chip away at the things obscuring your Great Work.

DEBRIEFING THE MAP

Take a minute or two to think about what just happened and what you learned by answering these questions:

▶ What was most interesting for you from this exercise?

▶ As you moved through the circles, where did your energy or excitement or interest increase? Where did it drop?

▶ What would be the cost to you if you didn't change anything and kept living with these irritants?

▶ Is there any connection between the various things that need to change? Is there an overall pattern?

▶ What do you know now about yourself that you hadn't fully realized before?

MAP 7

What's Required?

Balance the competing demands of your life

MOST OF US WORK FOR AN ORGANIZATION. And with that come conflicting goals and objectives.

Sometimes—rarely—all the planets are aligned, and everything we want to do is exactly what our organization wants us to do. But for most of us most of the time, there's a tension.

There's what our organization expects us to do: some of it Great, much of it Good, some of it, to be blunt, Bad. (Those reports, that meeting, this project. You know what I'm talking about.) And then there's the Great Work we know we could do if our talents and passions were fully recognized and realized.

The challenge is to find the best possible balance between these competing forces, so you are doing not only what is required and desired by your organization but also as much Great Work as you want.

That's no easy task.

I care

They don't care

They care

I don't care

Many of us default to just plowing through our in-boxes, processing what seems to be a nonstop stream of tasks and projects, big and small.

This map helps you to recalibrate, to delineate your priorities and those of your organization, so you can clearly see where they align—and where they don't. That's all in the service of helping you be clearer about what choices you can make so you can do more Great Work while still keeping your organizational masters happy.

COMPLETING THE MAP

1. **Bring to mind—or jot down on a piece of paper—all the work you do on a daily or weekly basis.** The more complete and more specific you can be, the more useful this map is. You might consider:

   ▶ Projects
   ▶ Parts of projects (for example, administration, finance, project management, team and departmental meetings, strategy, brainstorming, implementation, etc.)
   ▶ Administration
   ▶ Financial management
   ▶ Regularly scheduled meetings, such as team meetings or update meetings
   ▶ Ad hoc meetings
   ▶ Dealing with customers and clients
   ▶ Dealing with colleagues
   ▶ People management
   ▶ Training and skill enhancement

   (This is not an exhaustive list. Add anything that's missing for you, and/or use other terms that fit your situation better.)

83

2. **Figuring out where your time goes is often trickier than it sounds.** Even though you're working forty-plus hours a week, it can be hard to recall what you do all day. If it helps, consult your calendar or time sheets. If you're really drawing a blank, put this map on hold for a few days while you record what you do. I bet there will be some surprises.

3. **Once you have a pretty comprehensive list, start plotting it all out in the four boxes of the map.** When you consider what "They" care about, bring to mind your boss and also your boss's boss. Consider their priorities. You'll find it's much easier to be clear about theirs than it is to pin down the organization's priorities (which will typically be too high-level and abstract to be useful for this exercise).

4. **In the top right box, map all the work your organization wants you to do that is also meaningful to you.** This will be Good Work and may also include some Great Work.

5. **In the bottom left box, put down whatever work you do that you really don't enjoy and, now that you think about it, your organization doesn't care much about either.** This will be your Bad Work or the work that is at the bottom end of the Good Work spectrum.

6. **In the bottom right box, write down all the work you don't really have much passion for but your organization expects to be done.** Like the box to the left, this one will contain your Bad Work or the work that is at the bottom end of the Good Work spectrum.

7. **Finally, in the top left box, put down the work that you do, want to do, or think needs to be done but that the organization doesn't value.** This area is typically high in Great Work with some Good Work.

GETTING INSIGHTS FROM THE MAP

Each quadrant suggests a certain approach to the work that you've listed there.

1. **You care and they care.** A sweet spot. This is probably Good Work for you and for your company and may include some Great Work, too. Certainly spend time here and seek out more work for this quadrant.

   It might also hold seeds of more Great Work. Look at what's listed and ask yourself, *What would it take to turn some of these projects or responsibilities into Great Work?*

2. **You don't care and they don't care.** This work is pointless. No one cares. Stop doing it. (That's one sure way to find out whether the organization really doesn't care about it.)

   If you can't stop doing it, figure out the minimal level at which this work can be done, and deliver it at that level. To spend any of your time doing this work one iota better than adequately is to waste your life. The very acme of pointlessness is doing this work excellently.

   > How we spend our days is, of course, how we spend our lives.
   >
   > *ANNIE DILLARD*

3. **You don't care, but they care.** This is work that has to be done—but not necessarily by you. Consider delegating it, either in whole or in part. If you have to do it yourself, look for ways to do it more efficiently or to diminish the amount of it. Here are two great strategies for doing that:

   EMBRACE ADEQUACY. Adequate means "good enough." Many of us are programmed to operate at top level for everything we do, so we overwork and overdeliver even on work that really doesn't require such dedication. We pay by losing the opportunity to do more Great Work.

EMBRACE LAZINESS. Lazy people are often extremely efficient, because they look for the fastest, easiest way of doing things. If you were lazy rather than conscientious, how would you approach this work?

4. **You care, but they don't care.** In this box, you often find Good Work and Great Work. Unfortunately, the organization isn't interested; here you and they are out of alignment. This is work you're doing or you want to be doing, but it's not getting the attention you think it deserves. That can make this the trickiest area to manage, and most commonly the way we do this is by just letting this work die a sad and lonely death.

Here are three strategies you can consider to keep it alive:

DO IT UNDERCOVER. Best summed up by the adage "It's better to apologize than to explain." Waiting for permission to do this work will leave you waiting forever, so go ahead and start it, get it partially done, and then see if anyone's interested. This is a classic strategy for making innovation happen in organizations.

> Efficiency is
> intelligent laziness.
>
> *DAVID DUNHAM*

RELABEL IT. Find a different way to present this work, so that your organization will recognize its value. You're trying to move it across into the "They care" box. Know what your boss's boss's three key priorities are, and then find a way to link this work to those priorities.

DO IT ELSEWHERE. Accept that you'll never find the time and space to do this work in your current role in this organization. So do it as outside work in your personal time. Or find a new role within the division or the company to which you could transfer and where you can do it. Or, most radical of all, find a new organization that wants you to do this work.

FOR EXAMPLE . . .

Janet was taking stock after two years of very hard work as a junior lawyer. Her new promotion was a perfect opportunity to step back, and we met her doing that in Map 3. On the surface, many things were going well. She was getting good feedback and encouragement, she was earning a good salary, and the job had a certain prestige.

But she was tired. She worked long hours but wasn't at all certain she was doing much Great Work. The previous maps had started to make more apparent the gap between what she did and what her strengths were.

Working through Map 7 helped Janet get clearer about just what she considered Great Work and how much of that could fit into her current role and what her law firm expected of her.

Here's how she filled it out:

They don't care		I care		They care
▶ Environmental law		I care	▶ Research into new areas of the law	▶ Two high-profile pro bono cases based on civil rights issues
▶ Staying connected with the other young lawyers	▶ Team building	▶ The one time I had to manage a team		▶ Client management, being point person for the client relationship
They don't care				They care
			▶ Most of the regular corporate client work	
▶ Two internal committees I am on	I don't care			▶ Time sheets and administration

As Janet reviewed the map, she realized that things perhaps weren't as grim as she had thought they were. There were some interesting "seeds" in the "I care and they care" top right-hand box, in particular the lines about how much she'd enjoyed managing a team and her role as point person for client relationships. They offered some good clues as to where she could find and perhaps grow more Great Work.

The "I don't care / They don't care" bottom left-hand box wasn't overly full. But she was suddenly aware that these two committees she was on were a waste of time for everyone. She'd be moving away from them as fast as she could.

Scanning the "I care, they don't care" box, Janet realized several things. First, she'd never have an opportunity to do environmental law here. It was just the wrong firm. If that really mattered to her, she'd have to change jobs. Team building was also something that was unlikely to happen much, although there were occasional opportunities and she'd have to keep her eyes open for them. Connecting with other young lawyers, though—that actually felt like something she could do. She even felt she could find a way to position it so it would be seen as useful by the firm. That would be fun, perhaps even Great Work.

The challenge lay in the bottom right-hand box. That contained the bulk of her work, most of what the firm was employing her to do. This was the big *Do I keep saying yes to this?* question she had to face. Or did she need to find a new role, a new firm, a new career?

BEYOND THE MAP

One thing that often happens as a result of this exercise is that you come to question your assumptions about what "they" really care about. It can be easy to assume that you know, without ever really knowing for sure.

To find out, go ask your boss (or if you're feeling a little braver, your boss's boss) just what her top priorities really are. Don't give her wiggle room. If she's a little abstract or high level about things, ask her what her top priorities are for the coming month. And if that still doesn't work, ask her about the next week.

Here are some useful approaches:

▶ "I'd like to understand exactly what matters most to you."

▶ "If you had to give me the bottom line on what our key goals are, what would it be?"

▶ "What are the challenges you're up against at the moment?"

Then ask, "And what else?" after every answer, until she doesn't have any more answers.

DEBRIEFING THE MAP

Explore the lessons of the map further by answering these questions:

▶ How did this exercise confirm what you already knew?

▶ What new insights did you get from this exercise? What were you surprised to see?

▶ What greater clarity do you have about what "they" want or care about?

▶ What greater clarity do you have about what you want or care about?

▶ What would you like to be different?

> A man is a success if he gets up in the morning and gets to bed at night, and in between he does what he wants to do.
>
> *BOB DYLAN*

How to Say No When You Can't Say No

One of the fundamental tasks on the path to doing more Great Work is figuring out what you want to say yes to. But you also have to decide when to say no. If you only say yes, you're just adding more to your plate—and I bet that's already close to capacity.

But it's hard to say no. Let's face it, some of us can't even say no to telemarketers. So how do you say no to people you work with, live with, and care about?

The answer is not to focus on saying no but rather on saying yes more slowly.

What gets us in trouble is that yes is our fast, default answer to any requests that are made of us. Sometimes that's the right thing to say. But sometimes you're being asked merely because you're the first person they thought of or because the request hasn't been thought through. Often, it's worth getting to yes a little more slowly. And here's how you do that:

1. Say, "Thanks very much for asking. Before I say yes, just let me make sure I understand what you're asking for."

2. Then ask some good questions. There are three basic types:

WHY ME?
- May I ask why you're asking me?
- Have you asked anyone else?
- Have you considered asking X? He's got some experience with this.

WHAT'S THE BRIEF?
- When you say "urgent," what

does that mean? When's the latest it has to be done by?

▶ How much time will this take?

▶ If I could do only part of this, what part would you like me to do?

▶ What does "finished" look like for this?

WHAT'S THE BIG PICTURE?

▶ Have you checked this out with my boss?

▶ How does this fit with our three key priorities for this week/month/year?

▶ What should I not do so I can do this?

If you use this approach, any of four things might happen.

1. The person will answer all your questions, and you'll be happy to say yes. (This doesn't happen very often.)

2. The person will say, "Good questions! Let me get back to you when I've got some answers." And they may or may not come back. Because instead . . .

3. The person may just ask someone who says yes faster.

4. Sometimes you'll be asked to stop with the questions and just do it.

Don't start with the toughest, most senior person you work with. Instead choose someone with whom you think the approach might work, and a project that's not too important. Practice the questions, and as you get more confident, use them in more situations with a wider range of people.

> That woman speaks eighteen languages and can't say no in any of them.
>
> *DOROTHY PARKER*

Here's the bonus: ask these questions more often, and you'll start getting a reputation for being a strategic thinker. That makes you a more valuable player in your organization, which already has enough people who know how to say yes quickly. ■

Ka-boom!

A FEW YEARS AGO, AN INTERNET VIDEO showed two guys putting on a spectacular show reminiscent of the Bellagio fountains in Las Vegas—using nothing but Mentos candy and big bottles of Diet Coke. You've got an equally potent set of perhaps unlikely-sounding ingredients ready to be combined in the quest to help you do more Great Work.

Through the information you've gleaned from Maps 2 to 4, you've got insight into who you are, what matters to you, and what your Great Work might consist of. Consider that your Mentos.

Having completed Maps 5 to 7, you now have an expanded sense of where opportunities for Great Work might lie—your metaphorical Diet Coke.

No doubt you're restless to move to the next step of the experiment—adding the two together. Perfect! The next step is to pick your Great Work Project.

PART 4

Pick a Project

Make a Choice

Yogi Berra, always a font of wisdom, is alleged to have said, "In theory, there's no difference between theory and practice. In practice, there is."

You can keep reading this book as a theoretical exercise, understanding the insights and exercises in principle but not actually doing them, not actually putting yourself on the line. Or you can step up and say *I do actually want to* do *more Great Work, not just read about doing it.*

If you take the second option (and I hope you will), then now's the time for you to choose a Great Work Project to work on for real.

You've got new insights into what lights you up and makes you tick and what's important to you. This is your internal focus—what's important to you. You've also got new insights as to where you might be able to direct your passion and your talents. This is your external focus, where your desire to make a difference finds a need for that difference out in the world.

Now, make a choice to start.

> Striving for perfection is the greatest stopper there is. It's your excuse to yourself for not doing anything. Instead, strive for excellence, doing your best.
>
> *LAURENCE OLIVIER*

DON'T WORRY

One thing that might keep you from picking a Great Work Project is the fear that you'll choose the wrong one. You can just see that bright spark of courage to do more Great Work doused by a bucket of cold, murky "It's got to be perfect, don't make the wrong choice" water.

Map 8 will help you choose your Great Work Project with confidence, and this will kickstart your commitment to Do More Great Work. But a more important thing to hold in mind is this: Your goal is *not* to find the *perfect* place to start. That might paralyze you, forever delaying action because it's not "just so." Instead, your goal is to find *a* place to start. Make your best selection for now. It's not as if this is a tattoo that will remain indelibly on your forehead for all eternity. Take your best guess and choose something that will enable you to say, *This will do for the time being. This has potential. This is a good enough place to start.*

MAP 8

What's the Best Choice?

This, that, or the other?

IN *THE PARADOX OF CHOICE,* Barry Schwartz describes an experiment conducted in a gourmet food store. Customers were given a discount voucher if they were willing to taste samples of gourmet jams. There were two versions of the experiment. In one, six varieties of jam were offered; in the other, twenty-four.

The version with the twenty-four jams attracted the most tasters—all those flavors!—although people tried about the same number of jams in both the tests. But here's where there was a telling difference: 30 percent of the people who tasted from the lineup of six bought jam, whereas only 3 percent of those who tasted from the twenty-four choices actually purchased a jar.

> To change one's life:
> Start immediately.
> Do it flamboyantly.
> No exceptions.
> *WILLIAM JAMES*

MAP 8: WHAT'S THE BEST CHOICE?

	Criterion #1	Criterion #2	Criterion #3	TOTAL SCORE
Idea #1				
Idea #2				
Idea #3				

WHAT YOU CAN LEARN FROM
STRAWBERRY-RHUBARB-GINGER JAM

You probably react the same way. There are 127 varieties of toothpaste at the supermarket, but—like Robin Williams fainting in the coffee aisle in *Moscow on the Hudson*—most of us get overwhelmed and paralyzed by having too many choices. *What if I make the wrong choice, and I'm stuck with it? What if I don't have all the information? What if I'm missing something?*

Of course, there are times when it's really obvious which is the best choice, and you know that from the start. Maybe that's the case right now, and you're really clear what you want your Great Work Project to be.

But maybe you have a toothpaste situation on your hands, what with all the work you've done in the previous chapters. In that case, now's the time to narrow your options and select a Great Work Project.

COMPLETING THE MAP

There are two parts to this process. First decide on the ideas and the criteria, then make your choice:

1. **From the work you've done on the previous maps, and in particular on Maps 5 to 7, you've probably got some options for your Great Work Project.** Some are possibilities you already knew about, which the exercises brought into sharper focus. Others might be new options that the exercises revealed as having potential. From these, pick between three and five possibilities for your Great Work Project. You are looking for options that have potential to offer you more of the stuff that matters. Don't sweat it too much—this is just your short list, and the purpose of this exercise is to pick out the one or two most promising candidates.

2. **Develop a range of criteria by which to judge these ideas.** These are the key considerations, according to which you'll narrow your choice. Here are some potential criteria to think about:

- ► It's easy to do.
- ► It would have the biggest impact on what I'm trying to do.
- ► I want to do it.
- ► It excites me.
- ► It's fun to do.
- ► It's the best use of my skills.
- ► It would have the biggest impact for the person that matters most (whoever that is).
- ► The boss would choose it.
- ► It's likely to find a senior sponsor.
- ► It would be fast to do.
- ► It's cheap.
- ► It's the most efficient use of resources.
- ► It's cool.
- ► It's aligned with the strategy.
- ► It fits with the corporate culture.

The first three on this list are ones I use all the time. I highly recommend them.

3. **Now winnow your list.** I've found that three key criteria is a good number to aim for, and five is probably the maximum you need. The criteria can be rational (delivers at least a 10 percent return) or emotional (makes me smile). It doesn't matter which criteria you end up selecting, so long as they're the ones that will lead to more Great Work.

4. **Now it's time to measure each option against the criteria you've selected.** Write down the first option, then rate it against each of the criteria you selected, giving it a score of 1 to 10.

5. **Repeat for the other options.** At the end of the exercise, each option should have a total, and the highest score wins!

6. **To add more flexibility to the process, you can give your criteria different weights.** You'd do this if some are more important than others. For instance, you might give your most important criterion a maximum of 20 points, your second most important a maximum of 10 points, and your third, 5 points. Play around until you've properly represented the relative importance of each. Once you've found the correct weights, follow the same process as set out in steps 4 and 5.

7. **Finally, after you've added the numbers and determined which idea has scored highest, check in with your gut.** Does this choice feel like the right one?

GETTING INSIGHTS FROM THE MAP

1. **One of the strengths of this exercise is that it can put reasons to your intuitive feelings about which option you want to choose.** It not only confirms your choice for your Great Work Project, but it helps make transparent to you (and to those you have to explain it to) why it's the best choice to focus on for now.

2. **But perhaps your winner somehow doesn't feel right.** Somehow you feel in your bones that it's just not what you were hoping for.

   In that case, there are two places where you can revise your map:

► **Your criteria:** Have you really chosen the criteria that matter? What have you left off the list?

► **Your ideas:** Maybe you haven't hit on the right idea yet. Spend some time generating new ideas, then put them through the same process.

FOR EXAMPLE . . .

Carlos, the accounting-firm partner, had worked diligently through all the maps in the book to this point. They had reminded him that he had an entrepreneurial and creative spirit and that tapping into it more might offer him the possibility for more Great Work. Map 6 gave him the powerful realization that the stuckness he was feeling was also happening to the firm as a whole and that perhaps his Great Work Project had something to do with shaking up things.

As he revisited his notes from the exercises, he started jotting down options for his Great Work Project. He found four that he wanted to consider more closely.

1. Create a new product or service that the firm could sell to current clients. This idea was sparked by the new-projects area of Map 5, and it would certainly push him to develop and practice the new-ideas side of him that was revealed in the "This, not that" exercise.

> It is our choices that show what we truly are far more than our abilities.
>
> *ALBUS DUMBLEDORE IN J. K. ROWLING'S* HARRY POTTER AND THE PRISONER OF AZKABAN

2. Target a new niche of customers. Carlos had realized when working through Map 6 that both he and the firm had gotten a little too comfortable with their solid, reliable client base. Maybe he could help the firm develop expertise in a new sector and add a wave of new clients. That option awakened his entrepreneurial side.

3. Try to reinvent or upgrade the relationship he had with some of his clients. They were perfectly pleasant, but as he thought about the "Deep, not shallow" line from his "This, not that" exercise, he could see that he could be more strategic in his thinking, more personal in his manner, and more of a trusted advisor for some of his clients.

4. Leave the firm and find a new place to work. Carlos was almost embarrassed to admit this as an option, but it had popped up when he worked on Map 7 and was thinking about balancing what he wanted with what the firm wanted from him. This felt radical and scary, but Carlos decided to put it up for consideration.

Carlos decided to stick to three core criteria, but he gave Impact more weight than the other two.

► It's likely to have impact and get me out of my comfortable rut (20).
► It's easy to do (10).
► It can be done quickly (10).

Carlos put the four ideas through the selection process, with these results:

	Impact	Easy	Quick	TOTAL SCORE
New product	11/20	5/10	5/10	21/40
New niche	15/20	6/10	4/10	25/40
Upgrade relationship	15/20	4/10	7/10	26/40
Leave firm	18/20	1/10	2/10	21/40

To test the results, Carlos compared the scores not just horizontally but also vertically. In other words, under Impact, he made sure that the spread of scores felt appropriate and that New Product was in fact least likely to have an impact on his complacency and that Leave Firm was most likely.

> In the long run, we shape our lives, and we shape ourselves. The process never ends until we die. And the choices we make are ultimately our own responsibility.
>
> *ELEANOR ROOSEVELT*

Carlos sat back and considered his completed map. The first thing he noticed was the rush of relief that he didn't have to leave the firm. That was a good thing; he really liked it there. What interested him next were the top two choices—developing a new niche and upgrading his relationships. The new niche felt like the bigger Great Work Project from the firm's perspective, but on a personal level upgrading relationships felt like the more powerful challenge.

He realized that he didn't have to pick just one to the exclusion of the other. He could keep both these choices alive as his Great Work Projects for now. Carlos suspected that when he got into the specifics of what needed to be done and how these Great Work Projects would play out in reality, the choice of where to focus—if he needed to make such a choice—would become clear.

BEYOND THE MAP

If it comes down to two choices, and you can't quite decide which one to put your money on, here's a simple process to try: Toss a coin, assigning one option to heads and the other to tails. As the coin spins in the air, notice whether it's heads or tails that you're hoping for. That's the option you want. After you've identified it, spend some time figuring out the reasons why it's your first choice.

A variation of this is to ask someone to make the choice for you. "I'm thinking of doing X or doing Y. What would you recommend?" If the person is smart, she'll avoid answering the question but might ask you some powerful questions and coach you to greater clarity. And at a minimum, she'll offer an opinion against which you can test your reaction as with the coin toss.

DEBRIEFING THE MAP

Deepen the insights that you gleaned from the map by answering these questions:

▶ What was most difficult about narrowing your list of ideas?

▶ What was most challenging about selecting the criteria? What does that tell you about what matters to you and your Great Work?

▶ How does it feel to commit to a Great Work Project?

▶ Was there any resistance to doing this exercise? What was at the heart of the resistance?

▶ Where else could you use this "making better choices" exercise?

Great Work Wisdom

TWO SIMPLE STEPS

BY LEO BABAUTA

I'm a minimalist when it comes to productivity. Here's the only system you need, in two steps:

1. FIND SOMETHING AMAZING TO WORK ON. Something really amazing. A project that excites you and will have a high impact on your job and goals and life. Work on it at the beginning of each day, so it doesn't get bumped aside by other things. If you can, return to it at the end of the day, then clear your desk and prepare all the materials you'll need so you'll be ready to go first thing in the morning.

2. HOLE UP AND WORK ONLY ON THE AMAZING PROJECT. This is the key. Clear your schedule for a chunk of time—maybe 30 minutes if that's all you can spare, an hour is better, and 2 or more hours are even better than that. Then clear away all distractions: Turn off notifications for e-mail, IM, Twitter, and anything else that might pop up or make a noise; switch off your phones and any other mobile devices; remove the clutter in front of you; and most importantly, disconnect from the Internet. If you know you can't resist these distractions, go somewhere where you can't bring them. Tell everyone you work with that you will be incommunicado for an hour or three working on an important project. If you can, make this a regular part of your schedule.

Once you've holed up, don't work on anything except the amazing project. Seriously. Resist any urges to switch tasks, check on something, or get up and talk to someone. Those urges will come up. They're like an addiction — you just have to get through them. Steel yourself and sit there breathing deeply until the urge passes. Then get back to work. ∎

Leo Babauta is the author of the bestselling book The Power of Less and the creator of one of the most popular productivity blogs, Zen Habits, as well as the minimalist blog, mnmlist.com.

PART 5

Create New Possibilities

The Rhythm of Creativity

I spent the early years of my career working in what would become the world's largest independent innovation consultancy. My job was to help our clients invent new products

and services, everything from new laundry detergent to new pizzas. (A suspicion that the world already had enough varieties of laundry detergent was one of the reasons I left.) Besides inventing stuff, we also trained people and organizations to be more creative. One of the ways we did that was to talk about rhythm.

There's a basic pattern, a rhythm, to the creative process, a backbeat driving the emergence of ideas:

Out. In.

Expand. Contract.

Diverge. Converge.

Create. Select.

You open up, expand possibilities, and have ideas (out, expand, diverge, create). Then you narrow your focus, close down options, and make a choice (in, contract, converge, select).

And repeat.

KEEPING THE BEAT

As you're reading this, I'm going to assume that you've picked something to work on, a Great Work Project to turn your attention to. Either you've defined it by working through the previous exercises, or you just knew what it was from the start. It doesn't really matter, just so long as you have that point of focus where we can begin.

If you already know how best to proceed and what your next steps should be, don't let me get in your way. Put the book down and get out there. I'll be waiting for you when you get back.

Otherwise, you might want to expand the list of possible ways to pursue your Great Work Project. You might be asking yourself, *What are my options? What's the best way I could tackle this?* That's what this section is about.

In Map 9, you'll learn a quick and easy way to generate new possibilities, ideas, and opportunities.

In Map 10, you'll tap the power of scenario planning—imagining different ways your story might unfold.

And in Map 11, you'll use your own courage to open up new opportunities.

MAP 9

What's Possible?

Find the idea-generator within you

CORPORATE BRAINSTORMING SESSIONS can be dispiriting, soul-sucking experiences. The call goes out, "Let's brainstorm this," and hearts sink. People trudge into the meeting room, and an hour later, they trudge out again with few good ideas but with a deep and abiding resentment about orders to be creative.

MOVING FROM SIX CRAYONS . . .

But we're all better than we think we are at having ideas, our experience at brainstorming meetings notwithstanding. We have ideas all the time, throughout the day, every day. But we could have better ones and have them faster if we could overcome some limitations.

First, we've gotten it into our heads that we're not so good at coming up with ideas. That's what "creative people" do, and we're certainly not one of them.

Second, we have a limited number of ways we generate new ideas. Often, it's just one way: We concentrate hard for a bit—and typically we give ourselves very little time at all—and hope that a new possibility will just appear in our brain.

And finally, we rarely give ourselves enough time and space to have new ideas. When we're busy and in the processing mode that Good Work seems to engender, it can be hard to stop, focus, and create the relaxed free time that good new ideas require.

> If you limit your choices only to what seems possible or reasonable, you disconnect yourself from what you truly want and all that is left is a compromise.
>
> *ROBERT FRITZ*

Because we're in a hurry, we often just grab the first half-decent idea that comes along, regardless of whether it's the best idea we could have. I call this "first-idea-itis." You've got this "disease" if you simply run with the first idea that:

► Is coherent enough
► Doesn't suck too badly
► Isn't too hard to do

It's a common condition, particularly in organizations where the rush is on to move to action as fast as possible.

. . . TO THE FULL NINETY-SIX-CRAYON EXTRAVAGANZA

This map will help overcome this limitation and expand your ability to have good ideas, which in turn will expand your opportunities to do Great Work. Generating new ideas about how to do your project (and evaluating them as you did in Map 8 and will again in Map 12) helps you get out of old patterns and figure out effective new ways of working.

COMPLETING THE MAP

Use powerful, provocative, creative questions to generate new possibilities. Bear in mind that you don't actually have to *do* any of these ideas. Having the idea isn't a commitment to action. This gives you the freedom to let your mind stretch, knowing it's OK to generate ideas that are difficult or even impossible to implement. The process sometimes leads to new insights and previously unexplored avenues. Expanding your range of options is the first part of the creativity rhythm, and your goal here is to go big and go wide. There will be a time when you narrow your choices—but not now.

1. **This first step is to shift gears mentally, because this may be a little different from your usual way of thinking.** Generating ideas in a focused way is probably not something you do regularly, so you may find it frustrating. Hang in there. Think of your creativity as a muscle and recognize that it may not be as strong as it could be with regular exercise.

   Remember, you don't need to keep your ideas realistic. In fact, I encourage you to have ideas that are improbable, impossible, illegal, or irresponsible. This isn't yet about deciding what you're going to be doing; it's just about expanding your choices. And often the slightly insane ideas open the door for some more interesting (and sane) ones.

   Become aware of that little imp in your head that says, *I'm not much good at this* or *Unless the idea is perfect, I won't own up to it.* Just recognize that it's there, realize that its voice is not the truth, and keep trusting the process and coming up with ideas.

2. **Start by reconnecting with your point of focus, your Great Work Project.** If you've done the previous exercises, you should have a sense of what this is. If you haven't, now's the time to figure it out. It's tough to have ideas

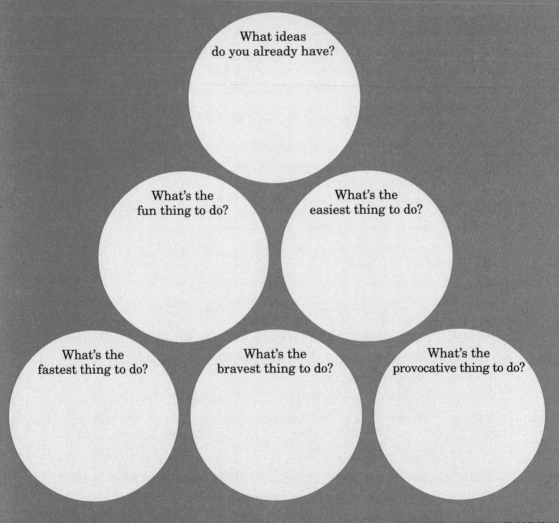

What ideas
do you already have?

What's the
fun thing to do?

What's the
easiest thing to do?

What's the
fastest thing to do?

What's the
bravest thing to do?

What's the
provocative thing to do?

if you don't know what you're having ideas about. Remember, choosing a Great Work Project isn't a do-or-die situation. This is likely to be only one of many such undertakings, and you can always change your mind or make adjustments along the way.

3. **Give yourself a time limit to have ideas (it's easiest to start small, say five minutes).** Then set an idea goal (three or four ideas a minute is an ambitious but doable goal, so you could start by aiming for fifteen ideas in five minutes).

4. **Start at the top of the map with "What ideas do you already have?"** This allows you to decant from your brain the current thoughts you have for beginning your Great Work Project. These ideas may be big and bold or small and tactical. They may be very specific or fairly abstract. They can be doable today or almost (or completely) impossible. You may also find that listing the ideas you already have leads to new ones. That's great! Write them all down. Keep going until you run out of ideas.

5. **Go back to the top of this list and reread step 1.** Remind yourself that some of your ideas will be half-baked, illogical, incoherent—or if you're really good, all three at once. This stage is about generating possibilities.

6. **Now you're ready to have some *new* ideas.** Scan the remaining questions and pick one that strikes your fancy. Whichever one catches your eye is a good place to start. Use it to generate at least three new ideas (or better yet, five). You might want to give yourself a time limit here, too, to help focus your mind. See if you can get your three to five new ideas in three minutes or less.

7. **Pick a second question and do the same.**

8. **If you're on a roll and have the time and inclination, pick a third question.** See what new ideas that generates.

9. **Review the ideas you've written down.** Did you hit your target number?

10. **As a bonus step, if you feel like it, pick your favorite two or three ideas and then springboard from them to generate additional ideas.** This taps into the rhythm of creativity—focusing on what's best and then expanding what's possible. One way of doing this is to speak out loud the idea you've already had and then add, "This makes me think of . . ." That phrase will help prime your brain to have ideas.

GETTING INSIGHTS FROM THE MAP

1. **Don't feel overwhelmed! You don't have to do anything with these— they're just ideas.** You've expanded what's possible, and it's entirely up to you which, if any, of these ideas you'd actually like to implement.

2. **Review all the ideas you've written down and take a moment to be proud of what you've accomplished.** Pay attention to which ideas look most interesting to you, but don't rush into choosing the ones you'll pursue. We'll get to that a little later. For now, stay open and increase your options. In fact, if reviewing what you've written sparks new ideas, add them to the list.

FOR EXAMPLE . . .

Things had moved quickly since Carlos had completed Map 6: What's Broken? and identified two possible opportunities for his Great Work

The Power of "And What Else?"

One of the most powerful coaching questions I know is also one of the simplest: "And what else?"

Its coaching power is threefold:

1. The first answer someone has is never their only answer and rarely their best one. This simple follow-up question allows all their other insights to come in out of the cold.

2. Asking "And what else?" stops you from leaping in and offering advice, a sure way to cut short an interesting conversation.

3. It gives you time to think of your next question. When you're struggling to know what the best question is to ask, saying "And what else?" buys you a little time. (It doesn't always work, of course, but it's worth a try.)

Don't forget that "And what else?" comes in a number of variations: "And . . . ?" "Can you think of anything else?" "Do you have any further thoughts on this?" They're all the same question with different makeup on.

The greatest gift is not being afraid to question.

RUBY DEE

"And what else?" also works beautifully in this exercise. The best way to decant your current ideas? Ask yourself, "And what else?" Pose one of the questions on the map; then when you've run out of answers, ask, "And what else?" You'll be surprised at what emerges. ■

Project: either to develop a new niche for the firm or to upgrade the quality of his relationships with some of his key clients.

He'd had meetings with the partners, and they had agreed—some more readily than others—that the firm was in a bit of a rut. The partners had debated the options before them: They could generate a new service, or they could amp up the sales process and find some new clients, with Carlos's idea of creating a niche being one way of doing that. In the end, they'd decided on finding new clients. It seemed to be the more obvious thing to do, and with Carlos willing to champion it and take the lead, they were happy to provide support.

> Everyone is a genius at least once a year. The real geniuses simply have their bright ideas closer together.
>
> *GEORG CHRISTOPH LICHTENBERG*

Carlos was delighted. His Great Work Project? Finding new clients, possibly in a new niche.

Turning to this exercise, Carlos decided to see what ideas he could come up with right away. He decided to aim for ten new ideas in ten minutes. He could have tried for more, but this seemed like a reasonable target.

The first step was to decant his current ideas. The first two or three came easily, because he'd been halfheartedly kicking them around in his head for years. He and his fellow partners could ask their current clients for referrals. Of course, they were already supposed to do that. But perhaps there was a way to create some sort of structure that would force him and everyone else to ask for referrals more systematically and effectively.

Another obvious idea he had was to take their services into a new market sector. They had no clients to speak of in the natural resources sector, and Carlos had a feeling that there was some opportunity there. Thinking about that gave him the idea of having one of the summer interns do some research on possible niches. Besides natural resources, he had two other possibilities in mind, and the research would help clarify whether it was worthwhile to try to establish the firm in one or more of them.

Finally, he thought he could get everyone to take a sales training course. No one in the firm had actually been trained in how to close a deal; they just sort of made it up, and it seemed to work well enough. Some added expertise might help. When Carlos asked himself, "And what else?" some other ideas popped up. Not great ones, he admitted, but he wrote them all down, knowing that they might spark new thoughts or turn into something better.

When he was drained of current ideas, he turned to the first of the provocative, creative questions: What's the easy thing to do?

Easy is good, Carlos thought. What were some easy ways to find new clients? Carlos could see how some of the ideas he'd already had fit that criterion, but the question suggested some other ways:

Call some of his friends—people in business but outside the accountancy world—and tell them he's looking for clients.

That made him think of calling his sister-in-law, who was a senior sales rep at a local technology company, and getting her suggestions about what to do.

Carlos's mind took a leap. He had a sudden flash that setting a "stretch goal" was a great motivator for him. One thing he could do that would be fairly easy would be to set a bold target for both the number of new clients and the amount of new revenue. Having a concrete target would help.

Finally, he could attend the natural resources conference that would be in town in a couple of months. That would be a great way to get a sense of what was really happening in this niche and whether there were any possibilities there for the firm.

Not bad, Carlos thought. It was almost odd that he hadn't come up with these in the "What ideas do you already have?" phase, but there were some real possibilities in that list.

He decided to pick one more question to help him get to his target of ten ideas: "What's the bravest thing to do?" Here are the ideas Carlos had:

► Stop client work for two months, so he could really focus on this challenge

► Jump in right away and aggressively pursue the natural resources sector

► Hire a professional salesperson to lead this initiative or to partner with him

This had been a more difficult question, but trying to get two or three extra ideas had pushed him. He wasn't sure if there was anything doable in that list, but it had certainly expanded his thoughts about what was possible.

It had been a productive session, even though it had taken only ten minutes or so. Some of the ideas had been more strategic about where to focus; some had been more personal about how to stretch himself in this Great Work Project. Both were interesting trains of thought. In fact, Carlos realized that it might be useful to get other people in the firm to go through a similar process with him, to expand the list of possibilities. He scanned the firm's internal phone list to see whom he might invite to join him for an idea-generating session next week.

BEYOND THE MAP

Go out and steal some ideas. (Tom Peters says you should replace the "not invented here" syndrome with the "stolen with glee" syndrome.) Here's how to do it. Take your challenge and go wander in your local shopping mall. Your goal is to find ideas, possibilities, and potential solutions to your challenge in what you see around you. This isn't about retail. It's about looking for new inspiration. Even though the connections may not be obvious, they're out there. A title in the bookshop might spark a new idea about how to manage one of your team members. How the clothes are displayed in a store might give you an idea for how to start a new project. The food court might inspire insight on how to reduce your busywork. When you're actively looking for new possibilities, you'll start seeing them all around you.

If you don't have a mall nearby (or you just want to avoid it), do this same exercise in a museum, in the periodicals section of the library, in a park, or anywhere you'd like. What's important is to leave your usual context, go somewhere new, and with your challenge in mind, look for solutions there.

DEBRIEFING THE MAP

Take a moment to let the lessons of the map sink in by answering these questions:

▶ What was it like to decant the ideas you already had? Did you have more or fewer ideas than you thought?

▶ Which were your favorite new questions? Which question produced the most new ideas?

▶ Was this process difficult or easy for you? Did you notice that imp, the "internal critic"? What was it saying about your ability to have ideas? About the quality of your ideas?

▶ How easy was it to have ideas that were illegal, immoral, or impossible? Did you notice a pull to stick to what's realistic? How did you manage that?

MAP 10

What's the Right Ending?

Explore different ways forward

THE SECOND OLDEST PROFESSION in the world, if not actually the first, is storytelling. Hunting stories are drawn on cave walls in France, Australian aborigines tell stories of the Dreamtime, and mythical stories are painted on Etruscan vases.

Mythologist Joseph Campbell said there's really just one story—the Hero's Journey—and its basic rhythm underlies all our tales, from Homer's *Odyssey* to Pixar's *Finding Nemo*. In fact, you can think of your life as a story with you as its hero. But stories are not just for bedtime, the fireside, or the pub. We can use the structure of the story to help generate new ideas and possibilities.

IMAGINE THIS

The smartest organizations have been using storytelling to help them make strategic decisions, only they call it *scenario planning*. In scenario planning, various ideas and situations are narrated, with happy and not-so-happy endings imagined and brought to life.

Visualization is a powerful human ability used by successful women and men in sports, business, and any part of life where goals have been set. As they imagine a future scenario—running their best 100-meter race and winning the gold medal, or wearing clothes that are three sizes smaller—they start imaging success and testing the route to that particular summit. As the saying goes, "It's not that you'll believe it when you see it, it's that you'll see it when you believe it."

What works for corporations and athletes can work just as well for you. One way to test possibilities is to give them a dry run by putting them into a story and visualizing where they lead.

The simplest structure for telling a story is the three-frame cartoon strip. In that strip you have the three basic building blocks of the story:

- ▶ **ONCE UPON A TIME** . . . where you set things up and introduce the hero (probably you).
- ▶ **SUDDENLY** . . . things shift, the challenge becomes clear.
- ▶ **AND THEN** . . . resolution! The way things work out in the end.

By telling a story, you can test possible Great Work scenarios. Storytelling is a way to visualize the future so you can make it more concrete. Playing out a scenario in story form can also enable you to see potential challenges, so you can adjust for them along the way.

COMPLETING THE MAP

1. **Bring to mind your Great Work Project.** You're going to imagine how it is going to play out, and you're going to tell three variants of the story. You

MAP 10: WHAT'S THE RIGHT ENDING?

Once upon a time...	Suddenly...	And then...

DOWNLOAD A FREE TEMPLATE OF THIS MAP AT WWW.DOMOREGREATWORK.COM.

can either write down the story in the three-box structure of the map, or if you're so inclined, you can draw it in true cartoon style.

2. **Your first story is the one in which things work out perfectly for you.** Everything falls into place. Everything you need shows up when you need it. You make all the right choices, and there's a happy ending. Tell that story in as much detail as you can, really imagining step-by-step how you arrive at the best possible outcome. It may be helpful to keeping asking yourself *And what happened next?* Resist the temptation to fast-forward to the ending without imagining the journey on the way. By describing the steps to success, you may generate even more good new ideas.

3. **Now tell a different story about the same challenge.** This time, imagine what happens if it all goes terribly wrong: all sorts of unexpected challenges get thrown in your way, you're continually thwarted, and it's nothing but a struggle. And the ending—not so great.

4. **The final variation is in the middle.** It's neither great nor terrible, just a mediocre experience. Nothing disastrous happens, nor is it a huge triumph. How does that story unfold? Again, fill in as much detail as you can.

The process of creating these simple stories will reveal new elements you need to consider, fears and expectations you may not have articulated, questions for which you may need to find answers.

GETTING INSIGHTS FROM THE MAP

Each story can offer you something to help you do more Great Work. As you tell the best-case story, you may begin to see the key choices you need to make, the important allies to get on board, the moments of truth that will make the difference. It's only by telling the story that these insights appear. Storytelling can also help you more clearly imagine what real, bold success looks like for this Great Work challenge.

The worst-case story can help you see where you might get derailed and what you're most afraid of. You may come to understand more clearly where the real challenges lie and how things might unravel.

And the ho-hum story, which I'm sorry to say is the most likely, can shed light on the regret and disappointment you might feel if you don't fully commit to the Great Work challenge. It can reveal how you might subtly sabotage your attempt to do more Great Work by playing it safe and small or by repeating familiar patterns of behavior.

You can drill down deeper and mine each of the three story sections for further insights.

ONCE UPON A TIME . . . Who are you as the hero? What qualities do you possess? Who else is there? What else is going on? What kick-starts this adventure toward more Great Work?

SUDDENLY . . . What's the real challenge? What are the barriers that you face? What might get in the way of success? How might you get in your own way?

AND THEN . . . How do you triumph (or not)? What does success look like? Failure? What needs to be in place for this to happen?

FOR EXAMPLE . . .

We last saw Sarika working through Map 4 and uncovering insights about herself as the starting point for where her Great Work might lie. She'd learned that there were two deeper truths about how she was at her best: being creative and working in partnership. When she looked into her past, when she imagined herself at her best, these were two themes that occurred again and again.

When she had internalized that insight and worked through Maps 5 to 8, she could see quite a few opportunities to do more Great Work with the company. In her new role as VP of IT, she was already seeing things with fresh eyes. There were projects that she wanted to start and processes that were broken and needed to be fixed. The difficulty would be in deciding what to focus upon.

She'd worked through Map 8 with Anton, a friend and mentor. They'd met for a drink after work, and he'd helped her look at her options and make a choice. In the end, Anton had helped steer her away from a project that emphasized doing things and turned her instead toward increasing her status and influence among her new peers. As Anton pointed out, she'd already impressed people with her technical abilities. She needed to develop new skills and a different type of relationship now that she was at this more senior level.

She was a little daunted by the challenge (in fact, that was one of the ways she knew it was a Great Work Project). She was younger than most of her colleagues at this level, she was a woman, and she was petite. It would be easy enough to let her voice go unheard or be dismissed out of hand. She had to make sure that didn't happen.

She worked with Map 10 to create three stories of how things would unfold. In the first, things went very well:

> The universe is made of stories, not atoms.
>
> *MURIEL RUKEYSER*

Fairy Tale

ONCE UPON A TIME . . . Sarika was smart, savvy, and strategic about how she worked on the senior team. She cultivated relationships with the three key influencers on the team (José, her boss, his trusted second-in-command, and the head of marketing), and she spent time with them outside the regular team meetings in a way that made it clear that she was capable of being a peer.

SUDDENLY . . . As the team faced a crisis during the rollout of an IT project, Sarika found the opportunity to assert herself. She offered a potential solution and brokered a deal between two of the team members that would help them collaborate better in sorting out the problem. She wasn't particularly involved in the details of the work itself; her role was finding the ways and means for her colleagues to cooperate and also providing some of the strategic thinking.

AND THEN . . . The solution played out as she'd suggested—hurrah!—and Sarika established herself as the "connector," fostering teamwork among the executives.

> There have been great societies that did not use the wheel, but there have been no societies that did not tell stories.
>
> *URSULA K. LE GUIN*

A Sorry Tale

She then looked at what might happen if things went badly.

ONCE UPON A TIME . . . On joining the senior team, Sarika decided the best thing to do was to play it safe: keep quiet, keep her head down and keep her nose to the grindstone, and hope things would work out well. She attended meetings, but didn't take a stand on much and just kept on doing her work. She kept most of her attention on her own team and her own project load.

SUDDENLY . . . The senior vice president and leader of the team took her aside and told her that she wasn't contributing as a VP but only as a director. That wasn't good enough, and the senior team couldn't keep carrying her like this.

AND THEN ... Sarika was demoted—or "moved sideways," as it was politely put—into a less important part of the business, and someone else was promoted into her position. On completing this story, Sarika was reminded to beware of catastrophizing (see page 171).

Neither Here nor There

Finally she told a story about things going just OK, neither well nor badly.

ONCE UPON A TIME ... Sarika played it safe during her first year on the senior team. Her job was to be neither too bold nor too timid and to prove herself with her work.

SUDDENLY . . . There *was* no "Suddenly . . ." She went to the meetings, had an opinion on some of the issues, hit her deadlines. She wasn't dismissed by her colleagues, but neither did she really establish herself as an equal among them. There was a sense that she was the junior member on the team and that she needed a few more gray hairs to really be credible.

AND THEN ... Years passed. Sarika was no longer on the fast track. She was in the middle of the pack. Eventually she was the old hand on the team, but her career had certainly slowed down.

Four things popped out for Sarika during this exercise. First, she found she didn't need a lot of detail in her stories. Even though she was painting them with a broad brush, they felt quite real.

Second, she didn't have to be influential with all twelve members of this senior team. Really, she needed to focus on just the three key people. That was a powerful insight, as she had only so much time and energy to give to building these relationships.

Third, she saw the danger in trying to prove herself by doing excellent technical work. That was what had gotten her on the team, but it wouldn't be anywhere near enough to make her a serious player.

Finally, she realized that she should play to one of her strengths—her ability to build relationships. Not only could she increase her own influence, she could add significant value to the top team by being a connector. Her other Great Work attribute—being creative—would find a place to be expressed. But it was in shaping and strengthening these influential relationships that success lay.

This was quite a shift from what she had been expecting to find. She had felt the strong need to prove herself by doing the work. But her Great Work actually was more subtle. By being influential at this level, she could help this senior team be more effective while also supporting her team to do their own Great Work.

BEYOND THE MAP

You can turn this exercise into a physical activity, and doing so has a curious effect. Telling the story while you move helps keep you from getting bogged down, and sometimes the details come more easily and more vividly. This exercise works really well with a partner. You can "walk the story line" together, and she can ask "What happens next?" to help you imagine the scenario.

Stand up, and find a place where you can walk in a straight line for at least ten paces. (A bigger space is better, but a ten-pace space will do.) Pinpoint specific starting and stopping points.

Stand at the starting point. The line before you represents the next twelve months, 365 days stretching out in front of you. Pick one of the three scenarios described earlier. Then start to walk along the line. As you go (moving as slowly as you need to), imagine what's happening at that time that fits with the scenario. By the time you hit the midpoint of the line, you'll be six months into the future, describing how your Great Work Project or challenge is going. You'll find it's easier than you think to imagine what's happening, and you may be surprised at what you find yourself saying. Remember, provide as many details as you can. The more detailed it is, the more useful it will be. Then use the debriefing questions to help you understand what you just learned.

DEBRIEFING THE MAP

To help you recognize and remember your insights from this exercise, answer these questions:

▶ Which of the three stories was easiest to imagine? Which felt most real?

▶ What do you now see as most critical for the success of your Great Work Project?

▶ Where does danger lurk?

▶ To successfully do Great Work, how does the hero (that's you) need to act? What does the hero (you again) need to avoid?

Great Work Wisdom

WORK DIFFERENTLY

BY CHRIS GUILLEBEAU

It can be easy to believe that doing Great Work requires great sacrifice—and that this sacrifice is not always proportional to the reward the work might bring. That's an assumption worth challenging. We can in fact do more Great Work by choosing to work differently. Here are a few ideas:

CREATE A MONOPOLY OF YOU. You may have heard about being special and unique as a child, but you can really start to apply the message as an adult. If the Great Work you do revolves around your unique skills and branding, then you have no competition. You are a market of one, set loose on the world to do Great Work that creates lasting value.

> You are remembered for the rules you break.
>
> *DOUGLAS MACARTHUR*

FOCUS ENTIRELY ON ABUNDANCE. Refuse to give in to the scarcity mind-set. You'll find that abundance and Great Work go hand-in-hand. Give more away, and share the credit for success. Build your work on positive emotions instead of negative. Continually think about how you can make others look good.

DON'T OUTSOURCE; JUST STOP DOING STUFF. If you feel overwhelmed and are thinking about outsourcing noncritical tasks, you can also just stop doing them. A good question to ask yourself is, "If I stop doing *x,* will my world come to an end?" If yes, you should definitely find a way to do it. If your world won't end, then there's an opportunity to take something off your "must do" list.

GIVE PEOPLE WHAT THEY WANT. Don't attempt to convince anyone of anything; recruitment is easier than evangelism. Instead of trying to convince people to see things your way, ask your customers and clients what they really want. Listen, not just to confirm your own biases, but to really hear what they want. Then find a way to give it to them.

AVOID (ALMOST) ALL MEETINGS. Very little Great Work comes from meetings. In fact, most meetings manage to kill off Great Work. Seth Godin is frequently asked how he has time to do everything, especially write back to everyone who e-mails him. His answer is that he doesn't watch TV and doesn't go to meetings, so that gives him four or five more hours a day than most people have. If you can't skip the TV, at least skip the meetings. (For best results, skip both.)

CHANGE THE RULES OF NETWORKING. Traditional networking involves scoping people out to see what they can do for you. Instead of asking "What can you do for me?" unconventional networking is externally focused. It asks the questions, "How can I help you? What can I do to tell other people about you? What are your goals?" The shifts from transaction to relationship and from taking to giving are two of the deep rhythms of Great Work.

Changing the way you work like this can help create an environment that (a) doesn't feel like work and (b) is centered on building real relationships. Do this, and you'll be on the right track to doing more Great Work. There's no waiting period; you can start immediately. ■

Chris Guillebeau *is behind the popular blog* The Art of Non-Conformity *and is the author of the popular (and free) manifestos, "A Brief Guide to World Domination" and "279 Days to Overnight Success." Chris's new book,* The Art of Non-Conformity, *will be published toward the end of 2010. You can learn more at www.ChrisGuillebeau.com.*

MAP 11

How Courageous Are You?

Take it to 11

IN THE HEAVY-METAL MUSIC MOCKUMENTARY *This Is Spinal Tap,* Nigel, the lead guitarist, shows off one of his amplifiers. It's the pride of his collection, because rather than the volume only going up to 10, this one goes to 11. As Nigel explains it, "When we need that extra push over the cliff, we put it up to 11."

In seeking ways to tackle our Great Work Projects, there are times when we could do with a little of that *Spinal Tap* magic (although there's no need for spandex or wigs, you may be glad to hear).

When we generate ideas, we tend to stay away from the dangerous edges where phrases like *highly unlikely, utterly unrealistic, totally unthinkable,* and *absolutely impossible* lurk. We scurry forth from the safety of what's known, daring to step a little over the line—but not too far.

This map is about nudging you toward that boundary, so you'll know what's just at the edge of what's possible—and what's over the edge. The exercise works particularly well in conjunction with Map 9. Together they're like a boxer's left-right combination, giving your idea-generating process some extra power.

COMPLETING THE MAP

1. **From the previous maps, pick a good, solid, safe idea you've had that would move things forward on your Great Work Project.** You don't have to overthink the choice; any solid idea that comes to mind will do. (If you've not done those other exercises—which is fine, by the way—think of an idea you've already got in mind for what you could do to take action on your Great Work Project.) Write that idea next to the 5.

2. **Now drop down to the 2 on the map.** What's the safest, smallest, easiest almost inconsequential version of that action? Write that down there. (We're going to assume that 1 means "do nothing at all.")

3. **Now jump up to 11.** What's the most ridiculous, possibly illegal, probably impossible thing to do? This is the "no boundaries at all" idea, the one to choose if consequences don't matter. Put your boldest, most extreme, most unlikely notion there.

4. **By the 8, write down a bold thing to do.** Choose something that's entirely possible but that would require you to pluck up your courage and take a deep breath. It should be like the idea you've written next to the 5—but with extra chilies.

> Be bold. If you're going to make an error, make a doozy and don't be afraid to hit the ball.
>
> *BILLIE JEAN KING*

135

11

10

8

5

2

0

5. And finally, at 10, write down your answer to this question: If you had no fear, what would you do?

As you complete this exercise, know that sometimes you'll generate variations on the same idea (call my mother, call my boss, call the CEO, call the president, call an election), and sometimes it will be a wide range of different ideas (call my mom, rearrange the office so I look out the window, stop working on project X, resign from my job).

Once again, please remember: You're not committed to doing any of these. You're just expanding your possibilities and exploring various avenues, so that when you do come to choose your action, you've got an excellent range of choices from which to pick.

GETTING INSIGHTS FROM THE MAP

One of the reasons why there's life on Earth is that our planet exists in what's called the Goldilocks Zone—neither too close to the sun so we burn like Mercury nor too far away so we freeze like Neptune.

> Great things are not done by impulse, but by a series of small things brought together.
>
> *VINCENT VAN GOGH*

This map helps you become more aware of your own Goldilocks Zone, which you sense only by bumping up against the boundaries of "too safe" and "too risky."

The goal of this map is to help you identify the most courageous idea that you'll actually implement, an idea that sits right on the edge of your courage and competence, at 8, 9, or 10 on the scale. You'll know it when you define it because your heart will beat a little faster and your hands might even sweat a little. You'll be both excited and anxious. In short, you'll know this is Great Work.

FOR EXAMPLE . . .

A ndy, who you remember is leading a marketing team to launch a new pharmaceutical product, had realized that his Great Work Project wasn't, as he'd thought at first, to create a brilliant marketing strategy, but rather to get his team working better.

The question was where to start? Andy could think of quite a few options, everything from the big-picture actions of resetting the vision and strategy for the team down to a whole host of smaller changes that might make a difference, such as increasing how often the team met in person or moving responsibility for certain parts of the project from one person to another.

But in his gut, Andy knew where he had to focus. He had to tackle the problem of Tom. Tom was a team member based in the U.K. and was something of an old-timer—over fifty with more than ten years at the company. Andy felt that Tom should have a good deal to contribute to the project, but so far he was proving to be, at best, a distraction. Tom's self-appointed role seemed to be to point out what wasn't working or wasn't going to work. And whenever he was asked to deliver something for the project, he claimed that his local obligations in the U.K. were more important and he could only partially contribute.

As Andy thought about Tom and what was going on, he recognized that he had contributed to the mess. Andy hadn't been clear enough about Tom's role on the team, nor had he challenged his disruptive behavior over the previous months. Rather, he'd just hoped that if he gave enough respect to Tom's

> Wanted: Young, skinny, wiry fellows not over 18. Must be expert riders willing to risk death daily. Orphans preferred. Wages $25 per week.
>
> *PONY EXPRESS ADVERTISEMENT*

seniority, the awkward situation would pass, and Tom would start behaving the way Andy wanted.

Andy framed his specific challenge like this: "Have a bottom-line conversation with Tom in which I firmly assume my leadership role and make it clear exactly what I want and expect from Tom on this team."

Working through the exercise, here's what he wrote down:

5: Send Tom a short "just the facts" e-mail setting out what the problem is and asking him to "raise his game."

2: Don't mention it and hope it all goes away.

11: Fly out to the U.K. with my boss, have a two-hour meeting with Tom, and give him detailed feedback in person.

8: Call Tom, do the usual small talk, eventually get around to the challenge at hand, and tell Tom I want him to be a better team player.

10: Draft a long, personal e-mail to Tom requesting a phone meeting about his role on the team, setting out the feedback I want to share with him, owning my own role in this problem. This will help ensure that I'm clear about what I'm asking for, that I treat Tom as an adult, and that I give him time to review the information before the call.

Writing down the options made it clear to Andy that it wasn't just an issue of calling Tom and saying, "Improve!" He had to thoroughly prepare for the conversation, so he could be really clear about what he wanted.

In fact, the process illuminated the next step for Andy—to go to his boss, Marilyn, and ask her to help him articulate the feedback he wanted to give Tom. He needed to identify not only what behaviors he wanted less of, but also those he wanted more of.

BEYOND THE MAP

Another way to tap into your courage is to step over the line and ask, *What wouldn't you do to move your Great Work Project forward?*" There's no doubt that there will be quite a few things on that list—things that are illegal or immoral, that go against your values, or that just feel beyond your scope. Write them all down. Once you've run out of things you wouldn't do, put the list aside.

Now it gets interesting.

However long your "wouldn't do" list is, your "everything else" list is much longer. You've come to the boundary between what you would do and what you wouldn't do from the other direction. Now you just need to find the bold ideas that didn't make the "wouldn't do" list and add them to your "could do" list.

DEBRIEFING THE MAP

Cement what you've learned by answering these questions:

▶ What do you know now that you didn't know before?

▶ What was it like when you moved from "possible—if I'm being very courageous" to "impossible"? What shift, if any, did you feel in your body?

▶ Did the insight about "playing it safe" ring true for you? Where else might you be taking the safer route?

▶ What would you be putting at risk if you were to take the more courageous route?

▶ What was it like to generate even more ideas about your challenge? Exciting? Tiring?

Your Body Leads Your Brain

Anytime you're tackling Great Work, it's worth considering where you're doing it—or more specifically, where you should *not* be doing it.

If you try to do Great Work at a place where you do lots of Good Work, you make life harder for yourself. Take your work desk as an example. As soon as you sit down in that familiar chair and look at that familiar desk with its familiar computer, you can feel your body and mind clicking into Good Work mode. You'll want to be focused, efficient, and productive, working on getting things done.

Great Work requires you to think differently, and one of the most powerful ways to help you think differently is to move differently. Even though many of us (myself included) tend to think of our bodies as transportation for our heads, neuroscience tells us that our bodies influence how we think and how we understand a situation.

Use that knowledge to create a different space for your Great Work. It could be anywhere. For instance, I have two desks in my office, one with my computer on it for Good Work and one that I keep fairly uncluttered and clear for Great Work. But you don't need two desks. Your Great Work space can be a meeting room, your kitchen table, a café, or even just a different part of your own desk. Just so long as it's a place where your body and brain don't snap into the "be efficient and process" groove.

Try it out. The best way to see if this is true for you is to experiment and see what it's like to do different types of work in different places. ∎

"Nothing Is More Dangerous . . ."

FRENCH PHILOSOPHER ÉMILE-AUGUSTE CHARTIER, better known simply as Alain, said, "Nothing is more dangerous than an idea when it's the only one you've got," pointing out the importance of generating new possibilities.

Too often when faced with a challenge, we seize the first idea that comes along and rush into action. This section has been all about slowing down, opening up possibilities, and expanding your options.

By creating possibilities, you give yourself choices. And with that comes responsibility—the responsibility to make the best choice you can. Sometimes the path is obvious and sometimes not. Sometimes the decision comes easily, but often it's difficult. In every case, however, making a choice is an act of independence in which you take, as author Peter Block puts it, "responsibility for your own freedom."

And now, if you're like most of us, you're itching to get going. Enough with the celebration of existential freedom—let's take action. That's exactly what the next section is about.

PART 6

Your Great Work Plan

Avoid Dust-Covered Dreams

If you've gotten this far, you have looked within and without, chosen your Great Work Project, and generated ideas to get your project moving.

Yet once again you are at a crossroads.

Do you stop here, your momentum shuddering to a halt as you put things aside and carry on with business as usual? Or do you push forward and turn possibility into action?

I'm making it a conscious choice for you, because it's so easy to get to where you are now—a challenge and some ideas on how to meet it—and then go no further. The intention is there, but the action is not. *I'll just get this project out of the way so I can start with a clean desk. I'll wait for my boss to be in a good mood before approaching her about it.* Time slips by, momentum is lost, you're still in your rut, and the project is not yet begun.

THE CHALLENGE OF STARTING SOMETHING

Even though having new ideas is difficult, it's also the easy part. At this point, it's all theory. No one's upset, no one has broken a sweat. But to commit to action creates consequences. You have to disrupt the status quo and stop doing something that's on your list now so you can start something new.

People are going to react, some positively and some negatively. You'll create a ripple in the universe.

It's so easy to stop at this point, to decide that this was an interesting thought-exercise, and if it was a different time or you were a different person or the circumstances were different, you could commit to doing more Great Work. If only you weren't so busy, if you didn't have myriad other responsibilities, or if the planets were aligned . . .

And so on.

But don't stop. Carry on. Do more Great Work.

MAKING PLANS

This section is all about pushing on, putting your plans into action, and making sure you do what you want to do.

In Map 12, you'll use four powerful questions to help focus your choice about what you'll do.

Map 13 helps you determine who might be able to help you on this journey, so you're not alone.

And in Map 14, you'll commit to action, figure out the next step, and take it.

MAP 12

What Will You Do?

Inspiration without action is just hot air

TOO OFTEN WE RUSH INTO ACTION before we should. In our organizations, there's an endemic, unspoken assumption that we must hurry, hurry, hurry at all times, as if busyness was a worthwhile goal in and of itself.

Much of what you've been working on up to now has been designed to slow you down a little. Who are you really, and what matters to you? Where might opportunities for Great Work be found? What is the right challenge for you, the best possible Great Work Project? What are all the options you could consider in terms of doing something?

The purpose of slowing down there is to speed up here.

Because now it's time to commit, to decide what you will do, and this map gives you a way to quickly narrow your options and decide what it is you will actually do.

1. What's the easiest thing to do?

2. What would have the most impact?

4. What will you do?

3. What do you want to do?

COMPLETING THE MAP

1. **This exercise is to help you choose an action you will take to get your Great Work Project underway.** To do so, we're going to narrow the field from the various possibilities you've created in the previous maps, so have a list of all those options on hand.

2. **Start by answering the question, "What's the easiest thing to do?"** Pick the simplest idea you've had and jot down the answer under that question on the map.

3. **Now answer, "What would have the most impact?"** Write down what would make the most difference as part of your Great Work Project.

4. **Now focus on, "What do you want to do?"** This is the idea you're most drawn to and most excited by, the one you've got the most juice for.

5. **Finally, you're ready to answer the question in the middle of the map.** But before you make that choice, spend a moment getting yourself into the best frame of mind.

   Take a deep breath. Close your eyes. Reconnect to one of those peak moments you recalled in Map 2 on page 32. That's going to help you remember what you're capable of and just how good you can be.

   Now think about what difference this Great Work Project will make in the world. Imagine the project being fully successful. Whose lives will it affect? What will be better as a result?

   Now that you've remembered just how good you can be and what difference this Great Work Project will make . . .

   Write down your answer to the question, "What will you do?" This is the action you're prepared to commit to, the action you're prepared to start.

GETTING INSIGHTS FROM THE MAP

The power of this map is that it chunks down your ideas in two steps. That helps make your final choice more considered and bolder than it might otherwise be.

In the first phase, you take all the ideas you've generated and define three outliers. "What's the easiest thing to do?" defines the bare-minimum step, something you'd find easy to commit to. "What would make the biggest difference?" is often the most challenging, boldest idea. It sets the bar for the stretch goal. And "What do you want to do?" helps you get clear on where your own passion and inclination would take you. It's always easier to do something you want to do.

With those three perimeter ideas established, you then move to the second part of the process: What *will* you do?

FOR EXAMPLE . . .

Carlos had generated a number of possibilities by working through Map 10. Now, he realized, it was time to commit to something and actually get going on his Great Work Project to win new clients for the firm. He worked through the steps of the process:

> When all is said and done, a lot more is said than done.
>
> *LOU HOLTZ*

1. **What's the easiest thing to do?** As Carlos scanned his ideas, it was quickly clear that the easiest thing would be to attend the natural resources conference. All he'd have to do would be to sign up and then show up in a couple of months. Easy, but not that useful in actually creating much momentum.

2. **What would have the most impact?** This was a more interesting question. Carlos played around with some answers and realized that a combination of ideas would have the most impact. If he significantly reduced his current client load and focused, say, 50 percent of his time on sales, that would have a good deal of impact.

3. **What do you want to do?** This question helped Carlos reconnect with some of the personal Great Work motivation that had started this whole process. He wanted to be something of an entrepreneur, not merely a salesman. It wasn't just about closing the deal; it was also about trying to start something new and build it up. Carlos realized that he wanted to build a new niche within the firm and grow it to something significant.

> Begin today! No matter how feeble the light, let it shine as best it may. The world may need just that quality of light which you have.
>
> *HENRY C. BLINN*

4. **What will you do?** Ah—actually having to commit! This wasn't easy, because Carlos could see various options for the way ahead. In the end, he decided to commit to three things: First, he would talk to the managing partner about reducing his client load. He'd start by asking for two days a week and would try to settle for one.

He'd devote two-thirds of that time to focusing on new business and referrals from current clients. He'd spend the other one-third exploring opportunities in the natural resources sector to make sure it had the potential he thought it did.

That led to the final thing Carlos decided to do. Besides talking to his current contacts about it, he would also get one of the associates to put some of his or her time into researching the sector, and doing a deeper analysis of the real opportunity.

BEYOND THE MAP

1. **Revisit Map 8 on page 98 and use the evaluating system there to set up different parameters to make your choice.** Did you come to the same decision? Did you gain any new insights?

2. **Decide what's non-negotiable.** If I had to identify a single coaching question that was at the very heart of doing more Great Work, it would be this: "What are you saying yes to? And by saying yes to this, what are you saying no to?"

   By making the full choice explicit—yes *and* no—you're forced to articulate the implications of your decision. This helps break the illusion that we can keep saying yes to more and more requests and opportunities when our plates are already full to capacity.

   To help yourself do this, steal a principle from the art of negotiation: Get very clear on what the bottom line is—that is, what's absolutely non-negotiable.

   Now think about what you're currently saying yes to (all your myriad responsibilities) and assign each commitment to one of three categories:

   ▶ It is absolutely non-negotiable. I must do this.
   ▶ It feels non-negotiable, but perhaps, now that I think about it, that's not true.
   ▶ I can say no to this. It's negotiable.

   The challenge in this exercise is to be absolutely certain that what you put into the non-negotiable pile is indeed non-negotiable. It can be easy to assume that everything's non-negotiable, that you have no choice and it's all obligatory. In fact, you do have a choice. There's likely a good deal you can say no to, and while you may not feel comfortable doing it, saying no opens up the possibility to do more Great Work.

DEBRIEFING THE MAP

Expand the insights of the map by answering the following questions:

► Which question was most powerful for you? Which one generated the most interesting response?

► What was most valuable about creating a short-list of possibilities?

► What did you notice about your reaction when you committed to an action? Were you excited? Anxious? Full of relief? Something else?

► What was most powerful about this exercise for you?

Great Work Wisdom

EXPECT NOTHING IN RETURN

BY TIM HURSON

One of the most insidious barriers to Great Work is the obsession with "results." This focus can often blind us to the very meaning of work itself—especially if the hoped-for results are misconceived. Though it's undeniable that result-driven work has produced useful outcomes, it's equally true that it often misfires badly.

In 1976 two U.S. economists, Michael Jensen and William Meckling, published a paper entitled "The Theory of the Firm." In it they argued that businesses suffer when the interests of managers are not aligned with those of shareholders. To rectify this, they proposed the theory of shareholder value, which holds that the main job of executives is to maximize share prices and that the best way to institutionalize this is to tie management compensation to stock prices. *Shareholder value* became the management mantra heard in boardrooms, shareholder meetings, and shop floors across the business world.

Unfortunately, the theory has serious flaws. It emphasizes near-term changes in stock prices ahead of quality, employee satisfaction, and perhaps most important, customer value. Lost in the cult of shareholder value is the true raison d'être of business—meeting real needs in the marketplace. Management by share price proved to be disastrous for scores of companies. Ask almost anyone who works in one of these organizations, and they will tell you that shareholder value is often an excuse for compromising the value and meaning of their work. The obsession to produce "results" frustrates the ability to do Great Work.

Contrast this with the story of Nicholas Fueni. When I knew him, Nicholas was seventy-two years old, a gardener, living under the oppression of South African apartheid.

Nicholas was the wisest, and perhaps the happiest, person I have ever known. Nicholas had found his Great Work. He knew every centimeter, above- and belowground, of the garden he tended. He knew its flowers, its animals, it soils, and its moods.

To Nicholas, the garden wasn't a result; it was an ongoing process. Not that it didn't have a result. It was incredibly beautiful in every dimension: It looked beautiful, it smelled beautiful, it harmonized with its environment beautifully, and it gave profound joy to those who experienced it. But that was not Nicholas's goal. His goal was to know, to really know, and then to bring out the very best of, the small plot of earth that was his Great Work.

Too many of us view our work in terms of results, rather than in terms of the beauty of the work itself. We don't raise our children for results. How many times have you seen children rebel because the results their parents had planned for them just weren't right? The best parents protect their children, nurture them, and guide them where they can, knowing that results come best if they are organic.

Great Work comes from the understanding that we are already complete. There is nowhere to go, nothing to do. The end of all our struggling, whether we are rich or poor, famous or obscure, is the same. None of us can escape it. The Greatest Work we can do is to follow the model of Nicholas Fueni. Love your garden, know it as well as you can, nurture it, make it the best it can be, expect nothing in return. Ironically, this simple formula produces the best possible results.

The opportunity to produce Great Work is around us all the time. You don't have to wait a moment to start. ■

Tim Hurson *is founding partner of ThinkX Intellectual Capital (www.ThinkXic.com), a firm specializing in helping groups maximize their ability to develop and implement innovative solutions to complex challenges. His recent book,* Think Better: An Innovator's Guide to Productive Thinking, *is in its third English-language printing and has been translated into six languages.*

MAP 13

What Support Do You Need?

Doing Great Work by yourself means it's not Great Work

IMAGINE YOU'RE WAITING FOR A FRIEND in a bar. Like me, you tend to fiddle with things, and you're playing with a box of matches. You pull out one match and try to get it to stand up on end. No luck, of course; it falls down.

So you pull out another match and try to balance one against the other. Still no luck. You can't quite get the two matches to stand upright.

Only when you pull out a third match can you get them standing—by leaning them against each other to make a little tripod.

WE ALL NEED HELP

We're not so different from the matches. To get the job done, we need support from those around us—family, friends, and colleagues. That can be a tough thing to really understand, as many of us have been brought up to emulate the rugged individual, the lone hero who does it all himself.

But this is one of the paradoxes. Great Work inspires you, enthralls you, pulls you forward—it's deeply personal. And yet almost certainly, you can't do it by yourself. Almost undoubtedly, you need additional resources or equipment or specific technical skills or a set of extra hands or maybe just some encouragement.

The good news is that with some looking, you'll find all the assistance you need. This map will help you figure out who in your network can in your network provide the emotional, technical, and political support that you need to do more Great Work.

COMPLETING THE MAP

There are three places to look for help:

1. **People who love you.** They will offer cheers, hugs, and unconditional support. Don't underestimate just how important and sustaining these are. Spend more time with these people, be they friends or family. Tell them what you're up to, enjoy their encouragement and support. It's fuel for the journey.

2. **People with skills.** We all know people who have technical expertise, whether it's in accounting, law, computers, coaching, entrepreneurship, carpentry . . . the list is endless. These are people who can provide things, do things, fix things, combine things, give advice, and in general make things happen. You can almost always find people to do essential work for you, or at least help you with it.

3. **People with influence.** They can open doors, grease rails, make introductions, and help you connect with people whose help you need.

MAP 13: WHAT SUPPORT DO YOU NEED?

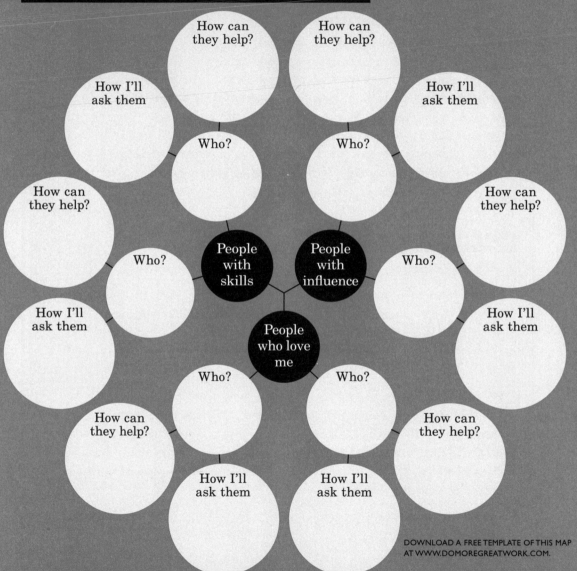

DOWNLOAD A FREE TEMPLATE OF THIS MAP
AT WWW.DOMOREGREATWORK.COM.

With your Great Work Project in mind, in the appropriate segment, write down two examples of each type of person and how they can help. (Sometimes one individual will fit in more than one category. That's fine. Put them in both or just one, whichever works best for you.)

Finally, decide how you're going to ask them for the support you need. You've got plenty of options. For instance, you could:

▶ Drop them a quick e-mail or post a request on a Web-based discussion board.

▶ Take them out for a coffee or lunch and ask them for advice.

▶ Ask them for a proposal, find out how much they cost, and hire them.

▶ Barter something you've got to offer that they might want.

▶ Ask if you can stop by and borrow their tools.

FOR EXAMPLE . . .

Sarika knew her current Great Work was to improve her influence within her new senior team, and in particular with the three members who carried the most weight.

> Everyone needs help from everyone else.
>
> *IVAN TURGENEV*

As she worked through this map to see who could help her with this challenge, she listed the following:

People who love me:

▶ Her partner, Louise, who's always there for her

▶ Her parents—ditto

▶ Her friend Mary, who also happens to be great at networking, so she might have some good ideas as well

Do More Great Work.

People with skills:

- ▶ Sue, a "transition coach" who specializes in helping people in the first ninety days of a new job
- ▶ Her former boss, Jason, who was brilliant at managing upward and could give her tips on how best to influence her current boss
- ▶ Mark, a communications coach who specializes in helping women get heard at the senior level
- ▶ Her hairdresser, who could give advice on a better style to fit her new role
- ▶ Her friend Carolyn, who has a great sense of how to dress in an appropriate, professional way

If you're a member of LinkedIn, Facebook, or Twitter, find me and get connected.

People with influence:

- ▶ The head of the team, José. Even though he was one of the three people Sarika was targeting, he could also be an ally. He was the one who promoted her, and he was already on her side. She could ask him for specific mentoring on how to improve her influence within the team.
- ▶ Kate, the senior vice president of human resources. Kate's not on this team, but she knows the others and could give advice and guidance on how to work best with them.

Sarika was most excited by the names in the second two segments. It would be easy enough to call Jason to ask his advice. And perhaps she could get the company to pay for some coaching with Mark. But the idea that most excited her was approaching José to ask for mentoring. It had the potential to kill two birds with one stone—better her relationship with him and also help her improve the way she worked with the others.

BEYOND THE MAP

With the rise of social media, the opportunity to expand the second category—people with technical expertise—is vast. Through Facebook, LinkedIn, Twitter, and the many other networks, you can now track down the best people in the world, not just the best people in your town. If you're not already a member, research these sites and decide which one is best for you. For instance, LinkedIn seems to be more about business networking; Facebook has a strong social bent (though more and more people are trying to use it to further their businesses); and Twitter is still trying to figure out what role it plays. Once you've signed up for a site, actively join the conversation. Lots of us have signed up with one or more of these sites but are very passive—members in name only. To increase the chances of a social network being useful for you, be an active participant. People are more likely to help you find connections if you've helped build and shape "the tribe."

DEBRIEFING THE MAP

▶ Does your network feel robust? Or a little weak?

▶ Who have you been underappreciating?

▶ Have you fallen out of touch with anyone with whom you should reconnect?

▶ With whom would it take the most courage to connect? (You could use Map 11 to find out.)

▶ To whom could you reach out and offer help?

> Sometimes I think we're alone in the universe, and sometimes I think we're not. In either case the idea is quite staggering.
>
> *ARTHUR C. CLARKE*

MAP 14

What's the Next Step?

Put the *Do* into Do More Great Work

YOU MAY ALREADY know this joke . . .

There are two types of people in this world—those who finish things, and . . . Don't be that second type. Don't let this trail off just when you're so close to action.

TWO SECRETS TO DOING WHAT YOU WANT TO DO

In his book *Getting Things Done,* David Allen shares a crucial insight: "You can't do a project. You can only do the next step." It's easy to get overwhelmed by the hugeness of a project, thinking, *Where do I even begin?* This is true with any project, and more so with Great Work challenges because often they're taking you into new territory. Deciding on, then taking, the next step is a powerful way to get moving. It's all very Zen. Take the next step. Then the next step. Then the next. And so on.

Map 14: What's the Next Step?

Another powerful way to keep your Great Work Project moving forward is to build in accountability. Consider these statistics on the likelihood of your reaching a goal you set yourself:

- ► 10 percent if you hear an idea
- ► 25 percent if you decide to do it
- ► 40 percent if you decide when you're going to do it
- ► 50 percent if you plan how you're going to do it
- ► 65 percent if you tell someone you're going to do it
- ► 95 percent if you set up a time to report back to that person on how you did

(I saw these statistics quoted as coming from the American Society of Training and Development, but I've never been able to satisfactorily confirm their origin. If you know the source, please let me know.)

Accountability is often managed poorly within organizations. Fear of conflict, fear of taking responsibility, fear of loss of face, and just plain lack of organization all contribute to cultures in which it's not exactly clear who is supposed to be doing what and by when.

It doesn't have to be this way. I believe most people want to be held accountable, because they do want to make good on their commitments. We've all felt the little sag of disappointment when someone doesn't call us on a promise we've made but haven't fulfilled. Yes, there's short-term relief. But there's also the disappointment that they broke their promise to follow up—and "enabled" us to do less than we wanted to.

> Traveler, there is no path. Paths are made by walking.
>
> *ANTONIO MACHADO*

In this instance, you're not having accountability imposed upon you; you're asking for it. You're at a point where you can choose to use it to support yourself

What will you do?

By when?

What accountability
do you need?

What's the first step?

or not. Make no mistake, deciding to build in accountability can be quite a daunting step. You have to find someone to ask. You have to be brave enough to share your Great Work goal. You have to be willing to swallow your pride and say, "I need help to do this." And you need to be clear on what support you need. This situation reminds me of the vulnerability expressed by William Butler Yeats in the poem "He wishes for the Cloths of Heaven":

> I have spread my dreams under your feet;
> Tread softly because you tread on my dreams.

No wonder it's so much easier to say, "I'll be fine. I can do this myself."

But Great Work is a difficult journey to walk alone. There's constant temptation to let yourself off the hook, to step back from being fully courageous. Then, too, there are the vagaries of fortune that threaten to stop you from completing your undertaking. Someone to help you over those hurdles can be invaluable.

Finding ways to create accountability doesn't involve demeaning yourself or putting yourself on a short leash. Rather it provides a structure to help you do what you want to do, to help you do more Great Work. In this exercise, I'll be pushing and encouraging you to set up an accountability structure.

COMPLETING THE MAP

1. **In the first segment, write down what you will do.** Make it clear and specific. It will have an action verb in it. ("Think about" or "try" and actions of that ilk don't count.)

    You'll know you've got a clear course of action when it's obvious what it will look like when you've completed it. If you can't define that, you don't have a specific action.

165

2. In the second segment, write down by when you will complete it. Be specific: Set a date and, if you need to, a time.

3. In the third segment, define the very first step that needs to be taken. Sometimes this will be the same as what you wrote in the first segment, but probably it will be a much smaller, more specific step, such as "Turn on the computer" or "Get Harper's phone number."

4. In the final segment of the map, decide whether you need support to be accountable to yourself. I urge you to seek a buddy.

Think about whom you might like to ask—a friend or colleague, family member, or peer. Ideally, it'll be someone you know who encourages you, but won't let you off the hook.

Get in touch and explain your Great Work Project and the action you want to complete. Then ask the person to ask you these five simple but powerful accountability questions:

▶ What will you do?
▶ By when?
▶ What does success or completion look like?
▶ How will you let your accountability buddy know you've finished?
▶ What are the consequences of not doing this?

Ask your buddy to check back in at the agreed-upon time (or times) to see how things have gone (or are going).

GETTING INSIGHTS FROM THE MAP

There's nothing tricky about interpreting this map. It's a straightforward plan for keeping you on the path to do what you want to do.

FOR EXAMPLE . . .

Janet had decided that for now, her task was to carve out more Great Work in her current job at the law firm. She knew that somewhere down the line she probably needed to think about finding a different job, but that time wasn't here yet.

Weighing things, it came down to two choices. First, try to reduce the amount of corporate law she was doing. It wasn't all Bad Work by any means, but she had come to see that this would only ever be, at best, Good Work. This wouldn't be easy. The firm had limited flexibility about who would do what work, particularly for the more junior associates. She could try to get more efficient at what she did, but it would be difficult to just stop doing that work.

> Hell, there are no rules here—we're trying to accomplish something.
>
> *THOMAS EDISON*

The second possibility was to focus on one of the opportunities she'd uncovered in Map 7 in the "I care – They don't care –" box: building connections with other young lawyers. This was something she had fun doing, and it tapped into one of the insights she uncovered about herself in the "This, not that" exercise in Map 3, in which she learned she was at her best when "Connected and networking, *not* Hiding and staying small." As an added bonus, this project even had the potential to help her with her future job hunt.

As she weighed the choices, the most enticing route had become clear: Her Great Work Project for now would be to build a "tribe" of other young lawyers.

By generating various ideas about how to actually do this in Map 9, Janet decided this tribe would be local to her city, would consist of lawyers in their first three years at work, and would be connected by various social media—Twitter, Facebook, and a dedicated website, as well as monthly in-person gatherings.

Great Work Wisdom

JAZZ AND GREAT WORK

BY MICHAEL PORT

Your capacity to do great things can never be measured by your talents alone.

Your work is only as great as your creativity, originality, and imagination—that's true. But there's another parameter. Your work is only as great as your collaborative spirit. It is your ability to collaborate that boldly and exponentially enhances your ability to put out head-turning, award-winning, publicly acclaimed work people won't soon stop talking about.

You must do "the work" yourself, but you shouldn't do it alone.

True collaboration is a beautiful balance of give and take. Helping yourself, you help others; they help you, and this unending spiral helps the world. It's like a circle, a roundelay, or a boomerang. It always comes back to itself in the end. It is one great, long jazz improvisation.

In jazz—that quintessential music of improvisational collaboration—players feed off each other. A theme on the piano becomes a riff on the guitar. The rhythm of the guitar becomes a drum solo. They make music together, music that moves the world and would never have been made singly.

Make it a point and a plan to surround yourself with expansive, like-minded collaborators. Experience the wonder of collective cooperation and find yourself doing far greater work than you could have alone. ■

Michael Port *has been called a marketing guru by the* Wall Street Journal *and an "uncommonly honest author" by the* Boston Globe. *He has written four books, including* The New York Times *bestsellers* Book Yourself Solid *and* The Think Big Manifesto. *Connect with him at www.MichaelPort.com.*

Map 14: What's the Next Step?

Janet was excited by the vision and had tested it with some of her friends at her law firm, who'd been excited, too. Now it was time to get down to the nitty-gritty of actually doing something about it.

There were plenty of places she could start. The first in-person gathering? Setting up the website? Finding others who might help organize this? Just spreading the word? She decided the best thing to do would be to organize a gathering in three weeks at a local bar. With that, she quickly completed Map 14:

What will you do?
Organize a gathering of young lawyers.

By when?
In three weeks.

What's the first step?
Finalize the date, time, and location.

What accountability do you need?
Working with my friend Mariella, who'll kick my butt if I don't do this now.

BEYOND THE MAP

If you *really* don't want to find a real-live person to support you, consider using stickK.com (yes, it's got a double K), a wonderful accountability tool. You'll register your commitment and set yourself regular periods to check in and report on progress. You can build a support team to monitor how you're doing. And you can put your money where you mouth is by putting cash on the line. If you reach your self-designated milestones, your money's safe. If you don't, it goes to a charity you've chosen. (Would you be more likely to do your own Great Work task if you had to pay, say, $5,000 if you didn't? I thought so.)

Do More Great Work.

DEBRIEFING THE MAP

Help the lessons of the map sink in by answering these questions:

▶ What's it like to be fully committed? (Are you fully committed? If not, what would fully committed look like?)

▶ How might you try to sabotage yourself from completing this task? What excuses do you think you might make for not getting it done?

▶ Who else could be part of your accountability group? Is there anyone else with the right combination of support and firmness?

▶ Where else can you use this structure in your life?

Face the Catastrophe!

One of the reasons we stop ourselves from taking a first step and doing more Great Work is because when we imagine moving forward, we become frozen with anxiety. In psychology, this phenomenon is known as *catastrophization,* a term made popular by Dr. Albert Ellis and practitioners of rational emotive behavior therapy (REBT), a form of cognitive therapy. Somehow, in a nanosecond, we move from one of opportunity to one of calamity. Here's a broad example of what it might sound like:

"I should speak up about my boss getting that detail wrong. It will take the team way off track, and we'll make a poor strategic decision.

But I could never challenge my boss . . .

. . . because she might get angry with me . . .

. . . and then she'd put me on nothing but bad projects . . .

. . . and then I'd fail at those projects . . .

. . . and then I'd lose my job . . .

. . . and I wouldn't find another one . . .

. . . so my wife would leave me . . .

. . . and I'd have to sell the house . . .

. . . and then I'd start drinking . . .

. . . and end up on the street, homeless, . . .

. . . dead before I'm forty-seven, . . .

. . . *and no one would even notice—* so maybe I won't mention her mistake after all."

It's almost humorous when you see it written down like this. Almost. But for many of us, this style of thinking is all too familiar. It paralyzes us. It keeps us small. ▶

171

It keeps us playing it safe and not taking chances to do something different, to explore something new, to do more Great Work.

BREAKING THE CYCLE

Do you tend to catastrophize? If so, it can be useful to watch yourself as you go through the process. Here's how you can do that.

I am an old man and have known a great many troubles, but most of them never happened.

MARK TWAIN

Pick an example from your own life that might trigger your catastrophizing. It might be about your Great Work Project, it might be "the most courageous thing to do" from Map 11, or it might be something else, something that pushes your buttons. Once you've written down the trigger activity, continue by writing down the whole catastrophizing process like the example I've given above. Doing this will make a difference, because you'll get a visceral sense of how absurd it is.

You can make the absurdity even more apparent by asking yourself, "Is that really true?" or "Is that actually likely?" about each one of the catastrophizing steps.

And if you really want to make the point, for each of the different steps, estimate the odds of that actually happening to you. For instance, in the example above, "she might get angry with me" might have a 20 percent (0.20) chance of happening, "she'd put me on nothing but bad projects" might have a 3 percent (0.03) chance of happening, and so on. You can then estimate the actual chance of the final catastrophe happening by multiplying the various percentages $(0.20 \times 0.03 \times \ldots)$. You'll end up with a vanishingly small likelihood that this catastrophe will happen to you. ■

The Tour de France

EVERY JULY, I SETTLE DOWN TO WATCH *LE TOUR*. My wife is mystified—how can I find it entertaining to watch endless hours of men in too much spandex?

One part of the race is the individual time trial. Rather than starting as a pack, the riders start two minutes apart, each with the goal of completing the course in the shortest time. Each rider goes through the same routine: He warms up on a stationary bicycle. Then, as his start time draws near, he wheels his bike to the start, a platform with a short ramp leading down to the road.

Finally, as the rider before him heads off, the cyclist sets up. He stands still, waiting to be released.

One minute to go . . .

Thirty seconds . . .

Then the final seconds are counted down:

Trois,

Deux,

Un,

And he's off! The pedals turn, releasing his pent-up tension . . .

And that's you. It's time to race.

Trois,

Deux,

Un,

Go!

PART 7

Continuing Your Great Work Journey

It Won't Always Be Easy

MAP 15 Lost Your Great Work Mojo?

Coaching Tip: Ac-cen-tu-ate the Positive

It Doesn't End Here

It Won't Always Be Easy

You've made a plan, and you're on your way to doing more Great Work. Bravo! This is no small accomplishment, and I hope you feel a sense of achievement. And I trust you've celebrated your progress in some small way.

I wish I could promise you that, having got to this point with focus, courage, and a plan, it will all be smooth sailing from here.

Sure, there will be times when things are flowing and you feel untouchable—focused, creative, and courageous.

But the very nature of doing more Great Work means there will be times when you stumble, times you lose the path, times when you're hacking through the jungle. You'll ask yourself if this was the right path in the first place. As various military leaders have pointed out over the years, "No plan survives contact with the enemy."

Here are some resources to help you get back on track.

Do More Great Work.

Map 15 helps you diagnose what might be going wrong and guides you back to various maps in the book that you can revisit to regain direction and momentum.

> Don't think of it as failure. Think of it as time-released success.
>
> *ROBERT ORBEN*

The coaching tip shares a number of powerful questions that you can use to reorient yourself when things aren't going exactly to plan—and things never go exactly to plan. They may help fend off any feelings of approaching doom.

Finally, the list of resources at the very end of the book directs you to additional insight, encouragement, and support you can tap into. I've included resources you can find at the www.DoMoreGreatWork.com website, as well as a list of the very best books and Web resources I know to expand your knowledge and your ability to do more Great Work.

MAP 15

Lost Your Great Work Mojo?

When you wander off the path

I LOVED WATCHING *THE MUPPET SHOW* as a kid. Reliable, long-suffering Kermit, the prima donna Miss Piggy, the insanity of Gonzo the Great. But I think my favorite character was Fozzie Bear, who told excruciatingly bad jokes but had a great tag line for all situations—"Wocka, wocka, wocka!"

Fozzie had a hard time of it. The two old guys heckled him from the balcony. People threw rotten tomatoes at him. Occasionally a long hook would appear from stage left and whisk him off into the wings.

But Fozzie was resilient. Next week, he was back with a new routine.

ROTTEN TOMATOES

Doing Great Work can attract rotten tomatoes. There are moments when you trip and fall. People are skeptical of your ideas. Corporate culture pushes you to shut down possibilities. There's an overwhelming amount of

179

MAP 15: LOST YOUR GREAT WORK MOJO?

Connect to why this matters to you
MAP 2, *page 32*

See how the journey might unfold
MAP 10, *page 124*

Move from fear to courage
MAP 11, *page 136*

Remember you at your best
MAP 3, *page 44*

Gain strength from your role models
MAP 4, *page 52*

Reconnect with your motivation
COACHING TIP, *page 57*

Review and reorganize your obligations
MAP 7, *page 82*

Check to see if you're catastrophizing
COACHING TIP, *page 171*

I'm confused or disoriented

I'm not sure I'm the right person

Recalibrate
MAP 1, *page 17*

I'm too busy doing too much Good Work

I think it's going to end badly

Imagine the best possible ending
MAP 10, *page 124*

Choose something to say no to
COACHING TIP, *page 90*

Commit to something
MAP 12, *page 148*

I've gotten stuck

I'm not sure this is the right project

Set up some accountability
MAP 14, *page 164*

Scan for better opportunities
MAP 5, *page 68, 70*

Reconnect with the essence of Great Work
page 5

Expand the possibilities
MAP 9, *page 114*

People are giving me a hard time

Review and weigh your options
MAP 8, *page 98*

Find a new space to do it
COACHING TIP, *page 141*

Define the next step
MAP 14, *page 164*

Connect back to yourself at your best
MAP 3, *page 44*

Ask for help from the right people
MAP 13, *page 158*

Find what's broken
MAP 6, *page 76*

DOWNLOAD A FREE TEMPLATE OF THIS MAP AT WWW.DOMOREGREATWORK.COM.

Good Work. You get pushback from your boss. Your inner critic sows seeds of doubt and encourages you to catastrophize. The list goes on and on.

Doing Great Work provides regular—weekly, daily, even hourly—tests of our focus and courage. To do more Great Work requires not just the bold act of saying, "This is my Great Work," but also the will to keep on doing it, even when the choice to not do it is often easier and more tempting.

This map helps articulate some of the slings and arrows of outrageous fortune that can prevent your doing more Great Work. It points you back to the resources in this book that can keep you on your intended path.

COMPLETING THE MAP

1. **Scan the map.** Notice where and how you are being pulled away from your Great Work. There may be more than one way; if so, pick the one you think is most distracting.

2. **Follow up and work through the exercises that the map points you toward.** This may seem like back tracking, but it will get you back on track and find new momentum. You'll find that revisiting the maps with new information and a new context will provide new outcomes.

> Failure is only postponed success as long as courage "coaches" ambition. The habit of persistence is the habit of victory.
>
> *HERBERT KAUFMAN*

GETTING INSIGHTS FROM THE MAP

There's a good chance that at some point in the course of doing more Great Work all of these bumps in the road—these moments of uncertainty, frustration, and confusion—will arise. That's why this map directs you back to

Do More Great Work.

the exercises you've already practiced. Revisiting the steps that got you here can offer new insights that will help you navigate the hazards and recharge your batteries. But what will most help you succeed to do more Great Work is determination, persistence, and a willingness to get back up again when you've fallen.

> Ever tried. Ever failed. No matter. Try again. Fail again. Fail better.
>
> *SAMUEL BECKETT*

FOR EXAMPLE . . .

Andy's conversation with Tom had gone well enough. It had been awkward, but sending the e-mail beforehand to set out the points he wanted to raise had helped, as had the coaching about the conversation that his own boss, Marilyn, had offered. He and Tom had stuck to the facts in the conversation, and Andy had been very clear about his expectations. Tom was still not contributing as fully as he might, in Andy's opinion, but at least he was no longer sabotaging the whole thing.

Nevertheless, the project was still limping along. Sure, he was doing a better job as the team leader in communicating what was needed and encouraging the group both as individuals and as a team. But it was still hard work, and the going was still tough.

Andy scanned Map 15 to see if it could help him figure out why it felt that things weren't quite clicking. Two of the ways Great Work gets derailed leaped out at him. The first was "I'm not sure I'm the right person." That was true: In those quiet moments when he wasn't working flat out, he kept thinking, *What am I doing in charge here?*

The second possibility was "I'm too busy doing too much Good Work." In truth, there weren't many quiet moments, because he was always in a meeting with someone or trying to catch up on his e-mail.

Andy went back to two of the maps to help him reorient himself.

The first was Map 7, the "I care/They care" map. The first thing he did was look at how he'd completed it the first time around. He was surprised to see that after less than three months, it felt a little out-of-date. He'd figured out both what he wanted and what was expected of him. Andy re-did the exercise, reflecting how things were now, and saw a few places where there might be opportunities to say no to some of his current workload. He decided to talk to Marilyn about getting himself removed from another project he'd been assigned. It only took three or four hours a week, but they were vital hours, and he needed to focus.

The second map Andy returned to was Map 4. The heroes exercise had been a powerful one for him, and he'd been able to bring to mind three role models who provided great guidance on how he wanted to show up in the world. When he reviewed the notes he'd made a few months back, what jumped out was one of the role models, Kate, a boss at his former company. Andy had really admired her ability to radiate confidence and clarity to the team. Even in tough times, she had a calmness and lightness that were very reassuring. Andy decided to "be like Kate" when he was feeling unsure of himself or uncertain about how to lead the team. He would figure out how Kate would handle the situation, and do it like that.

BEYOND THE MAP

When you get stuck, when you feel lost, it can be useful also to remember the five Great Work truths presented in the Great Work Movie (www .GreatWorkMovie.com). These are five fundamental principles about doing Great Work that you've heard me repeat, in one form or another, throughout the book.

Do More Great Work.

▶ **GREAT WORK TRUTH 1:**

Things only get interesting when you take full responsibility for the choices you make.

When things go wrong, it can be easy to slip into victim mode, proclaim that it's all too difficult, blame "them" for how it's gone haywire, and lie down.

Or you can acknowledge the situation, realize that you're still writing this story, and that if you're still alive, it's not yet over, . . . and get clear about what choices you're going to make.

▶ **GREAT WORK TRUTH 2:**

To do more Great Work you must both narrow and broaden your gaze.

When things aren't going as well as they might, it is valuable to reconnect with what matters to you. What's pulling you forward? How does this honor your values?

It's also wise to gain some perspective. Step away from the all-absorbing details in front of you, and reconnect with the bigger picture. Where's the goal? What are your other options? What really matters?

> Few things are impossible to diligence and skill. Great works are performed not by strength, but perseverance.
>
> *SAMUEL JOHNSON*

▶ **GREAT WORK TRUTH 3:**

Decide what to say no to.

What will you say yes to?
What will you say no to?

You must make the full choice.

Often what pulls us off the path is that we lose some of our focus and become overcommitted to other goals, distracted by other options.

Get clear on what the big yes is for your Great Work. Be bold about what you have to say no to.

▶ **GREAT WORK TRUTH 4:**

Stop making everyone happy.

If everyone's happy, then you're not doing Great Work.

It's difficult to do more Great Work when everyone else—the company, your boss, your colleagues, your team—seems to come first.

Part of getting clear on what you're saying yes to is that you're also getting clear about who might be a little disappointed by what you're saying no to.

▶ **GREAT WORK TRUTH 5:**

Ask for help.

Great Work is not a solo act. You need to draw on the wisdom, experience, and compassion of those around you.

When you're feeling lost or stuck, ask for help. It's tough to do this all by yourself. You might need technical help. You might need wheels to be greased. You might just need a cheerleader.

One way or another, you'll need support. Ask for it.

You can see these Great Work truths played out in living color at www .GreatWorkMovie.com.

Do More Great Work.

DEBRIEFING THE MAP

One last time, expand on the insights of the map by taking a moment to answer these questions:

▶ What pulled you off the path of Great Work?

▶ How might that be part of a familiar pattern?

▶ What was most useful about the solution to get you back on track?

▶ What can you do differently to break the pattern?

Ac-cen-tu-ate the Positive

When things are going less than perfectly, we tend to pay most attention to what's not working. To prove my point, just think of your last performance review. Let's say it was 95 percent good and 5 percent bad. And what hooked you? The 5 percent.

Sometimes it's absolutely appropriate to focus on what's not working and try to fix that. But two schools of thought among psychologists suggest that the secret to change is not focusing on trying to fix what's broken, but rather focusing on what is *working* and trying to amplify it.

WHAT'S WORKING WELL?

Before you moan, "It's all going wrong!" step back from the situation, take a breath, and ask yourself what's going well right now.

- ► What's working?
- ► What am I doing well?
- ► What are others doing well?
- ► What parts of the project are moving forward?
- ► What progress have we made?

The effect of such questions can be twofold. First, they can remind you that a good deal *is* going well; you can take heart in that. They also can serve to help you recognize exactly *what* is working so you can determine how to do more of that. This is often a more productive use of your time and energy than trying to fix what's underperforming.

Second, the answers to the questions provide a bigger picture for you, so that even if you do return to what's broken, you get to see it in context. That way, it doesn't seem quite so overwhelming. ■

It Doesn't End Here

I FIND GETTING TO THE END OF BOOKS like this one curiously anticlimactic and sometimes even a little sad. They can trail off and peter out or try to end with Something Inspirational (and often Slightly Bombastic) from the Author.

It feels to me that there should be some sort of celebration, or perhaps just a handshake: We look into each other's eyes and I wish you well as you set off on your journey to do more Great Work.

That's more to the point, I think.

Getting to the end of the book is just the beginning of it all. The really interesting things begin now as you find, start, and do more Great Work.

Safe travels. And come back when and if you need to.

P.S. PASS IT ALONG

Seth Godin is one of our leading thinkers about what makes work matter. Here's an excerpt from a blog entry he wrote in May 2008 about making the most of business books:

> It's not about you, it's about the next person. The single best use of a business book is to help someone else. Sharing what you read, handing the book to a person who needs it . . . pushing those around you to get in sync and to take action—that's the main reason it's a book, not a video or

a seminar. A book is a souvenir and a container and a motivator and an easily leveraged tool. Hoarding books makes them worth less, not more.

An effective manager hands books to her team. Not so they can be reminded of high school, but so that next week she can say to them, "Are we there yet?"

So if you found this book useful, don't put it on your shelf and never look at it again. Pass it along to someone else you think it might benefit.

P.P.S.

love feedback, regardless of whether it's good, bad, or indifferent. You can contact me directly at Michael@BoxofCrayons.biz.

More Wisdom and Inspiration

The Best Things in Life Are Free

Deepening Your Knowledge

The Best Things in Life Are Free

I'M A SUCKER FOR THOSE CHEESY TV ADS, the latest and most notorious being ShamWow! Remember the line, "But wait, there's more!"?

Well, when you buy *Do More Great Work*, you get the book. . . . But wait, there's more! We've got a bunch of additional tools I'd love you to access and use on DoMoreGreatWork.com, most of which are free and instantly downloadable.

The Free eCourse. Once a week for thirteen weeks—an investment of no more than three minutes each week to keep the insights and learning and motivation fresh over ninety days.

Map Templates. All the maps in this book are downloadable as full-page templates.

Map 16. An additional Internet-only map to help you find your Great Work.

The Great Work Interview Series. A series of interviews featuring inspiring leaders and thinkers from business and beyond. You'll find thought leaders such as David Allen, Guy Kawasaki, and Marshall Goldsmith; business leaders from organizations such as General Mills, PricewaterhouseCoopers, and ING Bank, and many others who bring their wise, inspiring, provocative take on Great Work. At the time of writing we've completed more than 90 interviews, and you can find them as MP3 downloads on the website and on iTunes (just search for "Great Work Interviews").

Deepening Your Knowledge

I'VE BEEN INFLUENCED by plenty of great writers and thinkers. Here is a deeply incomplete list of some of the resources that have inspired me, either directly or indirectly. I consider all of them to be not just good but great.

ABOUT COACHING

- Biswas-Diener, Robert, and Ben Dean. *Positive Psychology Coaching: Putting the Science of Happiness to Work for Your Clients.* New York: Wiley, 2007.

- Jackson, Paul Z., and Mark McKergow. *The Solutions Focus: Making Coaching and Change Simple.* London: Nicholas Brealey, 2007.

- Ludeman, Kate, and Eddie Erlandson. "Coaching the Alpha Male." *Harvard Business Review,* May 2004.

- O'Neill, Mary Beth. *Executive Coaching with Backbone and Heart: A Systems Approach to Engaging Leaders with Their Challenges.* San Francisco: Jossey-Bass, 2000.

- Rock, David. *Quiet Leadership: Six Steps to Transforming Performance at Work.* New York: HarperBusiness, 2006.

- Rock, David and Linda J. Page. *Coaching with the Brain in Mind.* New York, Wiley, 2009.

- Whitworth, Laura, Henry Kinsey-House, and Phil Sandahl. *Co-Active Coaching: New Skills for Coaching People Toward Success in Work and Life.* Palo Alto, CA: Davies-Black, 1998.

ABOUT HOW ORGANIZATIONS WORK

- Collins, Jim. *Good to Great: Why Some Companies Make the Leap . . . and Others Don't.* New York: HarperBusiness, 2001.

- Hock, Dee. *Birth of the Chaordic Age.* San Francisco: Berrett-Koehler, 2000.

- Law, Andy. *Open Minds: 21st-Century Business Lessons and Innovations from St. Luke's.* New York: Texere, 2001.

- Senge, Peter, C. Otto Scharmer, Joseph Jaworski, and Betty Sue Flowers. *Presence: An Exploration of Profound Change in People, Organizations, and Society.* New York: Broadway Business (Crown), 2005.

ABOUT FINDING WHAT MAKES YOU TICK

- Buckingham, Marcus, and Donald O. Clifton. *Now, Discover Your Strengths.* New York: Free Press, 2001.

- Cashman, Kevin. *Leadership from the Inside Out.* Provo, UT: Executive Excellence, 1999.

- Kashdan, Todd. *Curious? Discover the Missing Ingredient to a Fulfilling Life.* New York: HarperCollins, 2009.

- Kegan, Robert, and Lisa Laskow Lahey. *Immunity to Change: How to Overcome It*

If you want an interesting party sometime, combine cocktails and a fresh box of crayons for everyone.

—*ROBERT FULGHUM*

195

and Unlock the Potential in Yourself and Your Organization. New York: McGraw-Hill, 2009.

▶ Richards, Dick. *Is Your Genius at Work? Key Questions to Ask Before Your Next Career Move.* Palo Alto, CA: Davies-Black, 2005.

▶ Robinson, Ken. *The Element: How Finding Your Passion Changes Everything.* New York: Viking, 2009.

ABOUT TAKING RESPONSIBILITY AND SELF-MANAGEMENT

▶ Allen, David. *Getting Things Done: The Art of Stress-Free Productivity.* New York: Penguin, 2002.

▶ Babauta, Leo. *The Power of Less: The Fine Art of Limiting Yourself to the Essential . . . in Business and in Life.* New York: Hyperion, 2008.

▶ Block, Peter. *The Answer to How Is Yes: Acting on What Matters.* San Francisco: Berrett-Koehler, 2003.

▶ Carson, Rick. *Taming Your Gremlin: A Surprisingly Simple Method for Getting Out of Your Own Way.* New York: Harper Paperbacks, 2003.

▶ Godin, Seth. *The Dip: A Little Book That Teaches You When to Quit (and When to Stick).* New York: Penguin Portfolio, 2007.

▶ Jensen, Bill. *The Simplicity Survival Handbook: 32 Ways to Do Less and Accomplish More.* New York: Basic Books, 2003.

▶ Kabat-Zinn, Jon. *Full Catastrophe Living: Using the Wisdom of Your Body and Mind to Face Stress, Pain, and Illness.* New York: Delta, 1990.

▶ Koestenbaum, Peter, and Peter Block. *Freedom and Accountability at Work: Applying Philosophic Insight to the Real World.* San Francisco: Pfeiffer, 2001.

- Mind Gym, *The Mind Gym.* Boston: Sphere (Little, Brown), 2005.

- Pressfield, Steven. *The War of Art: Break Through the Blocks and Win Your Inner Creative Battles.* New York: Grand Central (Hachette), 2003.

- Rosenberg, Marshall B. *Nonviolent Communication: A Language of Life.* Encinitas, CA: PuddleDancer Press, 2003.

- Scott, Susan. *Fierce Conversations: Achieving Success at Work & in Life, One Conversation at a Time.* New York: Viking Penguin, 2002.

- Zander, Rosamund Stone, and Benjamin Zander. *The Art of Possibility: Transforming Professional and Personal Life.* New York: Penguin, 2000.

ABOUT CREATIVITY

- Hurson, Tim. *Think Better: An Innovator's Guide to Productive Thinking.* New York: McGraw-Hill, 2007.

- Tharp, Twyla. *The Creative Habit: Learn It and Use It for Life.* New York: Simon & Schuster, 2003.

- Vullings, Ramon, Godelieve Spaas, and Igor Byttebier. *Creativity Today: Tools for a Creative Attitude.* Amsterdam: BIS, 2009.

AND OTHER THINGS THAT MAKE ME THINK AND WONDER

- Arden, Paul. *Whatever You Think, Think the Opposite.* New York: Penguin Portfolio, 2006.

- Bryson, Bill. *A Short History of Nearly Everything.* New York: Broadway (Random House), 2003.

- Chödrön, Pema. *When Things Fall Apart: Heart Advice for Difficult Times.* Boston, Shambhala, 1997.

Do More Great Work.

- Gladwell, Malcolm. *Blink: The Power of Thinking Without Thinking*. Boston: Little, Brown, 2005.

- Guillebeau, Chris. *A Brief Guide to World Domination: How to Live a Remarkable Life in a Conventional World*. Seattle: self-published, 2008, free download from http://chrisguillebeau.com/3x5/a-brief-guide-to-world-domination.

- Kielberger, Craig, and Marc Kielberger. *Me to We: Finding Meaning in a Material World*. New York: Fireside (Simon & Schuster), 2008.

- Peters, Tom. *Re-Imagine! Business Excellence in a Disruptive Age*. New York: DK (Dorling Kindersley), 2003.

- TED: Ideas Worth Spreading, www.ted.com, a brilliant collection of eighteen-minute talks.

- Zeldin, Theodore. *An Intimate History of Humanity*. London: Sinclair-Stevenson (Reed), 1994; New York: HarperCollins, 1995.

About the Author

MICHAEL BUNGAY STANIER is the founder and senior partner of Box of Crayons (www.BoxOfCrayons.biz), a company that works with organizations and teams around the world to help them do less Good Work and more Great Work.

He was the 2006 Canadian Coach of the Year. He was also a Rhodes Scholar at Oxford University, and holds a Masters of Philosophy from Oxford, and law and arts degrees from the Australian National University.

Michael's first book, *Get Unstuck & Get Going . . . on the stuff that matters* (www.GetUnstuckAndGetGoing.com), is an award-winning self-coaching tool. Leading management thinker Peter Block says it has "a quiet political message in it that coaching is available to all of us and is not a profession but a way of being with each other." Michael also created the "Big Questions Trilogy" (www .BoxOfCrayonsMovies.com). These three short Internet movies—*The Eight Irresistible Principles of Fun, The Great Work Movie,* and *The 5¾ Questions You've Been Avoiding*—have been seen by well over a million people in at least 175 countries.

Michael regularly speaks at business and coaching conferences around the world. He also delivers Box of Crayons programs to private clients.

Prior to founding Box of Crayons, Michael held senior positions in the corporate, consultancy, and agency worlds in the U.K., the United States, and Canada. He has been involved in numerous large scale organizational change efforts, including writing the global vision for GlaxoSmithKline.

Michael grew up in Australia and lives in Toronto, Canada.

BOX OF CRAYONS

Box of Crayons' clients range from AstraZeneca to Xerox and are based in North America, Europe, Asia, and Australia. The company has expertise with blue-chip organizations in the professional service, pharmaceutical, and consumer goods market sectors. Its services include:

Do More Great Work Workshops. We offer a range of ways to bring the ideas of this book alive in your organization, ranging from one-hour teleclasses to full-day workshops.

Coaching for Great Work Program. A practical program to give managers and leaders practical coaching skills.

You can learn more at www.BoxOfCrayons.biz.